your dad
stole my rake

your dad stole my rake

and other family dilemmas

tom papa

St. Martin's Press 🐾 New York

www.stmartins.com

Designed by Steven Seighman

The Library of Congress Cataloging-in-Publication Data is available upon request.

ISBN 978-1-250-14438-6 (hardcover)
ISBN 978-1-250-14439-3 (ebook)

Our books may be purchased in bulk for promotional, educational, or business use. Please contact your local bookseller or the Macmillan Corporate and Premium Sales Department at 1-800-221-7945, extension 5442, or by email at MacmillanSpecialMarkets@macmillan.com.

10 9 8 7 6 5 4

For my family

contents

husbands

wives

pets

grandparents

the outlaws

brothers & sisters

aunts, uncles & cousins too

strangers

introduction

I want to thank you for reading the introduction to this book. I know you'd prefer to jump right into it, so good for you. Good reading. I'm hoping it's just as funny as the rest of the book and I'm feeling pretty good about our chances, so here we go.

In many ways this book is mostly about you. I'm not sure if we've met. I'm Tom, but even if we haven't, I want you to know that I've really been thinking a lot about you and I have to say, you're doing great.

I mean it. Everyone feels like they should be doing more with their lives, that they're not good enough or skinny enough, smart, rich, or successful enough. I get it, but stop beating yourself up already. You're doing fine. I'll go one better and say that you're peaking right now.

You really are. If you're living your busy life, dealing with your family, figuring out what to feed them next, and you were still able to find a couple minutes to read this, and enjoy yourself, this is as good as it's going to get. You're not stuck under a truck tire, no one needs to throw you a rope from a helicopter. Trust me, you're killing it.

It's hard being a person. It really is. Just the physical maintenance of you alone, is endless. Just the brushing, cleaning, and wiping—hopefully every day—of you, is a major project. Throw in the needs of the rest of your family and things get really tricky. So stop beating yourself up. You're doing great.

This isn't to say that your life is struggle-free. Everyone has their battles to fight. There may be slight differences in what they are, but no one lives a life without them. There will be sickness, money problems, and clogged toilets, but that's okay, it's all part of the package, so don't be a baby. As my grandmother would say, "Get over yourself!" You do the best you can, try to remember to floss, and have some laughs along the way.

The main source of these laughs is the people around you. Like you, I didn't choose the people in my family, but I knew from an early age that these people were hilarious. After performing, traveling, and meeting all of you, I've learned that your families are hysterical too.

Now, I know you're busy with all the important stuff you have to do. You have to draft players for your fantasy league, get your toes done before that thing you have to go to, so maybe you don't have the time to recognize what exactly makes your family so ridiculous. That's okay, that's my job. It's all I do.

That's why I wrote this book. To point out some of the absurd things that you might have missed and help you realize that you're not alone. We're all doing the best we can and that's truly enough. I hope you enjoy it.

Look at that, you got through the introduction! Nice job. You're doing great!

your dad
stole my rake

moms & dads

My parents are dumb. That's what we all think at some point in our lives. This is what makes it possible to break away as adults and go out into the world to do our own dumb things, like trips to Vegas, collecting mason jars, and doing shots of tequila with Don from sales. But just because we discover that our parents are mere mortals, doesn't lessen the impact they have on us or make our relationship with them any easier.

Our parents are the critics of our lives. Whether they're still living and leaving incomprehensible voice mail messages or they have moved on, finally relieved of their duties, it is their simple offhand remarks about what you were wearing or why you lost the spelling bee that will forever rattle in your head, with more devastating impact than a bad New York Times *review on opening night.*

Of course, parents don't realize their power because, from their point of view, no one ever listens to a single, solitary word they say. But children hear everything and the stuff that sticks is the stuff that is said without thinking.

My parents started their family when they were twenty

years old. *That seems impossible today, considering people in their twenties are lying on airport floors in their pajamas, Snapchatting their lives away. But it really happened. If I had known how young my parents were at the time, I would have responded to any demand that I clean my room with loud, laugh-track laughter, more commonly used on my siblings.*

I try to take their age into consideration when I reflect on the insensitive things they said or did while I was growing up, like the early Saturday morning when my father and I were driving along on Route 17. I was twelve, so I was probably rambling on about something important, probably having to do with Eddie Murphy's Gumby impression on Saturday Night Live *or the kid in school who accidentally blew off all his facial hair with a homemade rocket, when my father turned to me and asked, "Are you going to be one of those guys?"*

"The kind of guy who blows his face off with a rocket?" I asked.

"No, one of those guys who talks all the time?"

As someone who went on to build a career doing exactly that, you could imagine how insulted I was. I remember thinking, As opposed to what other kind of guy? A guy who sits alone in the den, in silence, watching nature shows and picking pistachios out of his teeth?

Of course I didn't say any of that, or engage him in any conversation at all, as it only would have helped bolster his point on the whole "talking guy" thing.

But I realize now that he was in his early thirties, having already burned his entire twenties being a family man, and was probably craving just a moment of silence in the car before he pulled into the parking spot of another place he didn't want to go, in order to do another thing he didn't want to do.

He shouldn't have said it, but I get it.

Eventually you go from judging your parents to being judged as a parent yourself. I had my children at an older age and even though I was wiser than I was in my late twenties, I still made major, moronic mistakes. For instance, when I killed my daughter's pet right in front of her. To be fair, I didn't know it was a pet, it was a snail she had found five minutes earlier, and I didn't intentionally kill it. I was happily walking up the driveway to say hello, when I heard something go crunch under my shoe. I tried to fix it but it turns out you can't scoop a squashed snail into a paper cup and expect it to survive. Not as anything resembling a snail.

While this may seem like a minor event, she is showing no signs of forgetting and continues to bring it up several times a year.

"Remember when dad killed Snaily?" she'll ask as if she's bringing up a murder that I am still doing time for. "I do," she adds.

Not only does she still remember, but I have a sneaking suspicion that this might be the opening to my eulogy.

It was an innocent mistake, with no ill intent, that will permanently be a part of my record. And that's the rap sheet for every parent. All the smart things you try to say, all the thoughtful lessons you try to impart, are eclipsed by the more memorable dumb moments in between.

So put your resentments aside, give them some respect for keeping you alive, and get through whatever phase of the relationship you're in, with the comforting knowledge that of course your parents are dumb. We are too.

no presents for dad

As the next holiday approaches—and it doesn't matter when you are reading this, a holiday is always approaching—I have some great news for you. You don't have to buy your father a gift.

That's right, you're off the hook. No more worrying about what Dad wants. Ever again. No more racing through the mall at the last minute, pricing out ties, looking at mini helicopters, and asking strangers what they got for their father. There is literally nothing he needs and nothing you need to buy. This isn't a fake "Aw shucks, don't worry about little old me" routine. This is real. He doesn't want a damn thing.

Think of your father as a clam. He has his house, he's in it, he's good. You wouldn't give a clam a new sweater with a snowman on it. He'd never wear it. Neither will your dad.

Sure, he needs the basics like deodorant, a toothbrush, and maybe some beer, but these aren't gifts, and only he knows the brands he likes and he's already bought them. He doesn't need you to try to improve on these items, either. He doesn't need a new toothbrush with bristles on the side or an extra arm that reaches teeth he didn't know he had.

He doesn't need you to change his unscented deodorant into "Arctic Ice" or "Courage" or "Pine Forest Adventure." He started using a deodorant in high school that smelled like menthol and he's sticking with it.

The same goes for his clothing. There is nothing that bothers a man more than opening a present and finding something he's now supposed to wear. He doesn't want to wear it. He already has the stuff he wears. But now he has to hold it up, pretend he likes it, and then secretly bury it in his closet alongside the other shirts with the tags still attached.

Let's face it, the reason he won't like what you buy is because you don't really know what your father wears. Think about it. What does he wear? It's probably not a question you've even thought about before. The universal answer is, "Who cares?" No one. No one cares what Dad is wearing. Maybe Mom cares when she wants him to make a good impression at church or dinner with the Haskells. He'll waddle out looking for his keys, she'll take one look at him, shake her head, and make him change. Two minutes later he comes back, in a slightly cleaner version of the same shirt, while she lets out a sigh and declares, "We have got to get you some new clothes."

But you really don't. If we were shooting a movie about your family the dad character would be fully developed. His costumes would have been picked, his haircut set, and his lines memorized. He is Dad. Dad doesn't need to be updated. Dad doesn't need to be brought into the future. Dad is Dad.

That's what we like about Dad. He's stable. He's a known thing. The kids are changing every day, evolving their tastes, trying things on, determining who they are. They could be an athlete one minute and be a black-clad emo kid the next. That's okay. That's expected. But not from Dad. Imagine if one morning Dad walked into breakfast with black lipstick and a dog collar around his neck. The earth would literally quake.

Even Mom is expected to change. A new hairstyle. New shoes. A new dress. Mom is all about change. If Mom isn't changing, there's something wrong. It's all she thinks about. She'll spend weeks talking with everyone she sees about dyeing her hair a new color. Eventually she'll do it, parade around with her new blond streaks for a day and a half, and immediately begin asking people for their opinion on her next big idea.

That's not Dad. Dad doesn't change his hair color. We want Dad walking into the room, a piece of hair sticking up in the back, in the same shirt he bought ten years ago, saying the same goofy dad greeting, and poking us in the neck from behind like he always does.

The real core of the problem with buying a gift for Dad is that it shows that we're thinking too much about this guy. Dad doesn't want this kind of attention. Dad doesn't want to be the focus. Sure, he wants to be loved and appreciated, but a hug once in a while is more than enough.

Dad doesn't want to create a hassle. Dad is about calm. Dad is about getting people to relax. He doesn't want you running around town yelling, "We forgot about Dad! What are we going to get Dad?"

He wants you to be home. He wants you to be happy. And, most of all, he wants you to leave him alone.

call your mother before she's dead

You should call your mother.

She's not kidding. Your mom really wants you to call. What if she dies tomorrow? This is really what she's thinking. What if she slips in the supermarket and gets caught in the ice cream aisle without a sweater and freezes to death next to Ben & Jerry's? What will you do then?

She raised you, fed you, and changed your diapers, which you wore for way too long, so it's the least you can do. Sure, she judged you but that's what mothers do. And, let's face it, you were a mess for a long time. During my whole Grateful Dead phase, when I grew my hair long and wore the same patchouli-soaked tie-dye shirt for a year, no one liked me. Only my mom.

So, call your mother.

You know, she literally sits by the phone for hours, staring at it, wondering where you are. What are you doing? Who are you with? What tramp is chatting in your ear? Your beautiful ears that should be listening to the most important woman in the world, your mother. You can always get another floozy, but you will never get another mother.

I'm not saying that making these calls is easy. It's a lot of work. A mother has very high expectations when her children call. My mother always acts like I just got released from a hostage situation.

"Thank God you called! Where have you been? I thought something must have happened. I was watching the news but they didn't say anything so I figured maybe you just forgot about me."

Technology hasn't made things any easier. Of course my mother is confused by the smartphone; the greatest technological advance during her childhood was the four-slice toaster. So, now, not only do I have to call her, I have to give her lessons that would stump even the smartest kid at the Apple Store.

FaceTiming with my mother is like watching a horror film when the zombie pops out of the lake, off the screen, and into your popcorn. It's all giant eyeballs, close-ups of lips, and screaming cries for help when she can't see us. When it does work it's even worse. Suddenly, my mother is right there in my kitchen. She's criticizing the meal my wife is making and asking me why she did that to her hair in a whisper that she thinks only I can hear. What makes it even scarier is that she insists on holding the camera directly under her chin, which, even for Emma Stone, is a bad angle. When my mother does it, it looks like she's trying to scare the children around a campfire.

"Delores said I should sign up for Snapchat," she screams into her phone. "I don't know what that is. Why? Why do I have to do that? I don't know what's happening!"

"Mom, you don't need Snapchat. Don't worry about that."

"Delores also says that her daughter is getting inappropriate texts from her boyfriend. How do I get some of those?" she asks, obviously on the second glass of wine.

It must have been simple when you could only call on a landline or, better yet, the pre-Edison days, when your only obligation was to write your mother a letter once or twice a year from your fishing boat. But it's not about us, it's about the moms, and it makes her happy to hear your voice.

So, call your mother.

Seriously, why fight it? You're no match for your mom and you know it. She is a cage fighter and you are a pink belt in thumb wrestling. She will wear you down, fill you with guilt, and stay in your head until you pick up the phone and call.

My mother has promised that if I don't call she will continue to haunt me even in the afterlife. They could offer her a FastPass to heaven and she will say, "No, thank you, I'm staying right here on this dirty earth, where I will follow my son to the end of his days."

So just do it, because when she's no longer here you'll be sorry. And there's a very good chance she could die tomorrow, because she has to go to the dentist and parking there is terrible and she could end up stuck in that underground parking structure until she is eaten by wild dogs that live in the dark.

Just call her.

tiger mom vs. ice-cream mom

There's been a lot of talk these days about the virtues of being a Tiger Mom. This is a mom who is as mean as a tiger. She has scary teeth and claws and stalks you as soon as you come home and she threatens to eat you if you don't get straight A's. She turns all of your *free* time into *go* time. Tiger Mom is fierce. Tiger Mom is mean. No one likes Tiger Mom.

Not only does Tiger Mom scare her own children, but she also scares other moms. The regular moms start to feel that just being a mom isn't good enough. Tiger Mom tells you that not only do you have to love your children, care for them, and make sure they're safe, but you also have to kick their asses like a drill sergeant at boot camp.

If that approach is in your DNA and you also enjoy kicking puppies and chewing on glass, more power to you. But if you don't want to run your house like an army barracks, I have a suggestion for you. Don't even try to be a Tiger Mom. Go the other way.

Be Ice-Cream Mom.

Ice-Cream Mom is the best! Kids don't see Ice-Cream Mom and cry. Kids get excited and scream her name, dance, and wiggle around. Because they know when they see her, there's a good chance they're getting ice cream. And everyone loves ice cream.

Kids love it. Parents love it. Your dog really loves it. Even angry, old people love it. I know people who are lactose intolerant who eat nothing but ice cream. Ice-cream cakes, ice-cream sandwiches. Ice cream makes people happy.

It's creamy, cold, and sweet, but taste is only part of it. The whole ice-cream experience is fun. Even the language around it is silly. Cone or cup? Sprinkles or jimmies? Chocolate sauce or caramel? How many scoops? This is silly stuff. Toppings? Who gives you toppings? Ice-Cream Mom, that's who.

When Ice-Cream Mom asks, "Who wants ice cream?" kids cheer, the dog wakes up, and Dad stumbles into the kitchen. With that one question, Mom just called it quitting time and threw the rule book out the window. It's a family safe zone. No one is going to yell at you during ice cream time. There will be no talk of homework or dirty rooms. The pressure is off and that's the point.

There is something forgotten when we talk about raising children: the fact that they're children. Ice cream is a break from all the work and discipline that is enforced all day long. And kids need a break. Sure, this is the time to teach them to excel and learn the right way to do things and be bold and strong and smart. But they also have to make a mess and lay on the floor and daydream. And what do kids daydream about? Ice cream.

The ice cream man served us well. For years he was the only option. Ice cream wasn't kept in the home. There was no Häagen-Dazs or Ben & Jerry's. When we heard that strange man in the rusted truck playing the spooky music we immediately started screaming and running in every direction at once. We all did.

Kids would come out of their homes, from under the slide, out of the woods, and down the street. Not organized; panicked. It was complete, unfiltered pandemonium. Kids would run smack into mailboxes, trip on curbs, and fall into sewers, but emerge with smiles on their faces because they were that much closer to ice cream.

I remember running toward that truck with such frenzied joy that I'd be fighting back tears. Blubbering, joy-filled crying. I'd get within two feet of his truck and only then realize I needed money and that I had none. Kids don't have wallets. They have pockets, filled with dirt and hair ties and chewed gum for later. We needed money and we needed it fast, and there was only one person who you could count on: Mom.

Eventually, with the help of the good people at the supermarket, she was able to cut out the middleman. Why should that weird guy without a high school diploma be the recipient of all that love? Thus, the birth of Ice-Cream Mom.

Is promising kids ice cream a type of bribery? Yeah, it is. That's the point. They'll do anything for a couple scoops. They'll do homework quicker, clean up after dinner, even fix up their rooms. You want your kid to practice their flute? Promise them ice cream. Want them to stop playing their flute? Promise them more ice cream.

My nana bribed us with candy that she kept in her purse. When she walked into the house we knew it was candy time. It was a real sign of love. She wasn't eating that candy. She wasn't walking around town chewing on Smarties. No, she carried that candy, day after day, because she knew that eventually she would see us and when she did she'd have candy. And we loved her for it.

I can hear Tiger Moms right now. I can hear them taking a break from oiling their shotguns, spitting out a wad of tobacco, and cracking their knuckles. They're calling me weak. How dare I suggest that we bribe our children with sweets? Sweets have sugar and sugar is a drug and it will affect their ability to study.

But I'm no fool. I won't fight you, Tiger Mom. You're right and I'm wrong. Forgive me if I'm not engaging in your arguments or paying attention to your points about human development. I'm a little preoccupied with this big bowl of ice cream, while happy children sing and dance all around me.

things you find on mom

Jeans That Used to Fit
Mom Sneakers
Food Stains
Hair Ties
Cheerios
Used Tissues
A Big Glass of Wine
Fisher-Price People
Smartphone with Cracked Screen
Xanax

don't ask your father

Everybody wants dads to do more. They look over at that guy slouched on the couch with his hand in his pants and think that he should be more involved. He should help with the children. He should plan the birthday parties, bake the cakes, and pick up the balloons. But let's be clear. Fathers aren't trying to avoid doing certain things out of pure laziness. There are some things that Dad isn't good at and the family is better off if he doesn't try.

I'm not trying to say that we should return to a time when fathers acted like a visitor to the home and the entire burden of the family fell solely on the mom. That families actually functioned that way without mothers killing their husbands in their sleep is shocking. But while there are plenty of things that Dad should do, here is a list of things that he should not:

put a daughter's hair in a bun.

I speak from experience. I tried. I really did. I wanted to do it, and do it well, and I could not. My daughter's strict Russian ballet teacher demanded that every girl come to class with her hair in a tight, professional-grade bun. Many young girls were brought to tears when the teacher humiliated them for a single runaway hair. That's nothing new. What was new was that my wife was out of town and I was left with the job of doing the whole bun thing. (That I call it the "bun thing" is not a great sign.)

I'd seen moms do it before. I saw my wife do it with one hand while driving the minivan with the other. How hard could it be? The answer: impossible. Hair isn't meant to be gathered into an orderly pile on top of your head. At least not by someone who doesn't even own a comb. When I was done wrenching my daughter's neck, pulling hair out of her head, and frantically jabbing her with pins, she looked like a demented voodoo doll.

I was soaked in sweat, not only from the physical effort but from the very real fear of what this teacher was going to do to my poor little girl. The only thing that stopped her from attacking my daughter like a drill sergeant who notices an untied shoelace, was that she noticed me standing in the doorway.

"Oh no. What did your father do to you? Girls, repeat after me. Dads don't do buns."

She was very wise.

do the laundry.

It's too much! I can't do it. I really can't. I wear the same jeans and black polo shirt every single day. I just can't spend the time in my closet worrying about what to wear. Einstein was the same way, but he had big things to think about. All I'm worrying about is my next joke about nachos, and still I can't focus.

So the idea that I'm going to care about, pay attention to, and treat with respect everyone else's clothes is out of the realm of possibility. I guarantee that if I'm in charge, your clothes will end up wrinkled, faded, shrunk, wet, moldy, and smelly. So I recommend that you do it yourself or head to J.Crew for some nice black polos.

dress the children.

Again, this is something I don't care about. They can dress any way they want as long as it doesn't become attractive to creeps. It's all fine with me. Let them express themselves. Sunglasses and a birthday hat? Sure. Overalls and clown shoes? I don't see why not. Seven layers of mismatched, stained, oversize shirts? Have at it. If it makes them comfortable and they don't mind being called names at school, then who am I to interfere?

feed the animals.

I only mean that I can't do this with the regularity, care, and expert delivery that my wife provides. She heats things in the microwave for them and cuts chicken down to bite-size pieces. I can only care for the pets as much as I care for myself. When I'm left on my own, my feeding schedule is erratic, the things I eat are bizarre, and some days none of it happens. So if you don't mind the dog living like a dog, I'm your guy. If you want the dog to dine like Beyoncé at Nobu, look elsewhere.

your children should at least *think* you might spank them

I have never spanked my children. It wasn't a plan, or some philosophy that I declared once we had them. We made these two little girls and as soon as I looked into their eyes I knew there was no part of me that could ever consider hitting them in any way. What a chump.

They're not perfect. They've ruined some furniture, some nights, and some vacations; irritating me in quick and surprising ways. They have also scared the hell out of me, doing all the dumb, dangerous, seemingly suicidal kid things. They've run into traffic, put a paper plate in the oven, and jumped into a pool with no idea how to swim. Sure, they've made me angry, but I still couldn't spank them.

Part of the problem is because they're sweet little girls. I know little boys start out sweet, but if I had a son, I could definitely spank him. I've hit every guy I've ever known—my father, all of my friends, coaches, priests—but never a girl. I slightly raised my voice to my daughter when she was misbehaving, and we were both so upset that we instantly got colds.

And yet, despite my opposition to spanking them, I'm not sure it's a good thing. I am a powerless leader. I'm not feared;

I'm laughed at, brushed off, and conned. When my wife threatens them with, "You just wait until your father gets home," they just laugh.

"That guy? Great, I'm running low on cash."

My daughters have turned this weakness into their advantage. It's a power vacuum that they have happily filled. They have more control over me than over anyone on earth and not because I love them, but because they play me like a fiddle. Make no mistake, they know exactly what they're doing.

My youngest came in and asked me for something. I denied her and she left the room to talk with her sister. A little while later she returned and, being only four, said out loud, "What if I ask like this?" as she batted her eyes, raised her voice to an angel's pitch, and put her hand on my arm. "Pleee-ase." She's a four-year-old con man, using methods perfected by her older sister, and I fold like a card table.

To replace spanking I have some minor disciplinary tricks like guilt and compassion that are somewhat effective. I can get quiet, act disappointed, and draw them in with my distance. But these are slow, tedious endeavors and have very little lasting effect. If only I could have raised my hand one time, had the courage for one spanking, I could have reclaimed my kingdom and ruled like the king I was destined to be.

My father spanked all of us kids, two sisters included, and we did not like it. Not at all. We were truly scared of him, and when my mother said, "Wait till your father comes home," it was a real threat that would send us running for the safety of the secret fort built inside our toy box.

But was it truly effective? It depends on what you're after. If it was an attempt to get us to learn more quickly, then I would say no. He could spank us all he wanted, but the fact is kids do dumb things for years without thinking about the consequences. My daughters are learning more quickly than I did and all without a sore behind.

But if it was a dictatorship he was after, then, yes, it was very effective. He sat at the kitchen table with his arms folded like Mussolini and everyone did as he said. When he said, "No," we knew that was the final word. At least until we asked our mother.

I am no Mussolini. I'm the deputy mayor of Girltown. Does this make me less powerful in their eyes? Does it make me seem soft and willing to do anything for them with just a little prodding? Yes, it does. But, at the very least, when they get older they'll never be able to write in a book that I was mean and scary.

I guess they could, but that would be a lie and for that I'd spank them for sure.

things you find on dad

Steak Sauce
A Lighter
A Swiss Army Knife
Pennies
A Flask
Screws
Bullets
Jerky
Fish Hooks
Excedrin

stop trying to be cool

I am a dad. That doesn't really tell you much. It tells you that at some point I spent some time with a lady friend, we drank some wine and made some people. But after that, there's not much you can tell because there are many, many ways to be a father.

A dad can be absent. A dad can be present. A dad can be strict. A dad can be doting. He can be an active part of the house or he can be as involved as the stuffed chair in the den. There are single dads, part-time dads, stay-at-home dads, sometimes two dads. There are dads who come and go. Dads who live down the street. And dads who never leave that one corner of that one couch.

He may be one of these things and he may be all of them. Being a dad is a fluid situation. I would like to focus, for now, on two types of dads: the Fun Dad and the Old-School Dad.

the fun dad

First of all, the Fun Dad isn't that much fun. He's annoying. He's the dad you see at the park in line for the slide. He dresses like his kids. He uses words that his kids use and he runs around a lot. This isn't a dad. This is a guy who's trying to reach back into the past and relive his childhood, only this time being more popular.

Fun Dad really wants the kids to like him. He is desperate for their approval and will stop at nothing to get it. He hangs upside down on the monkey bars, fills up water balloons, and buys everyone a round of juice boxes.

The problem with Fun Dad is that, much like a party clown, he'll be amusing for a little while but everyone will eventually grow tired of him. The kids slowly realize there's something desperate and creepy about this guy and they slowly drift off, leaving this grown man playing alone in the sandbox.

At least Fun Dad is trying. It's admirable that he really wants to participate, but the family pays a price. If he's all fun, then who do we turn to when the car breaks down in the middle of the freeway?

the old-school dad

I like this guy. He may be crude and a little off-putting. He may be too strict and not hold much respect for people, other than himself, but this guy is a rock. He stands strong and declares confidently what is right and wrong.

The era of black-and-white certitude may be over, but not for this guy. He doesn't wallow in the gray area. He says things like, "My way or the highway," "Because I said so," and "I'll give you something to cry about."

I know it sounds a little harsh today, but there's a clarity to this guy. He's old school because he's from a different time, when a father wasn't compromised by what people thought of him. He didn't care about being popular, he just cared if everyone in the family was okay, and if they weren't, he would do something about it.

You know where you stand with Old-School Dad. Everyone does. There are rules. The kids know they can't curse at Grandma, the dog knows he can't jump onto the couch, and the cat knows if he claws the sofa, there will be hell to pay.

I know it's cool to act like complete freedom is the way to go, but it's not. We need order. Life has too many options and without some clear guidelines and limits, we end up making dumb choices and having to call home looking for bail money. Old-School Dad keeps us in line.

For a child, it's calming to know that there are no choices for dinner and that they get what they are given. It allows their brains to relax and work on other things. When Old-School Dad tells his children they can swim for twenty minutes, not a second more, the kids know what they're dealing with because Old-School Dad has a history of scooping them out like salmon if they try to fudge the clock.

Everyone knows that Old-School Dad means what he says and says what he means. We may not agree with his rule against eating pretzel rods in his car, but it is one less gray area to get lost in.

Old-School Dad is a good guy to have around during a fight. Old-School Dad doesn't let strangers get close to his family and he'll blow if he sees a dog without a leash coming their way. Old-School Dad isn't quiet about it, either. He'll yell at the guy to get a damn leash, he'll yell at the dog to back off, and then he'll turn to his own kids and tell them to stop acting like morons.

He's not perfect, by any means.

He has road rage and a very low tolerance for other people. Especially people in front of him on lines, working behind counters, pumping his gas, standing in the aisles of the food store, talking too loudly at the table next to him, boarding an airplane, trying to hail a cab, or just being alive and in his way.

But despite his faults, I choose Old-School Dad. He provides order and stability in an insane world. He won't be doing flips inside a bouncy castle, but that's okay. That's what children do.

children

If you're lucky, you just might fall in love, get married, and build a peaceful, happy home. A quiet place where the two of you can relax in harmony, for the rest of your days. Unless, of course, you decide to have children, at which point your home will be invaded by the worst roommates you could possibly imagine.

From the minute they show up, your life is no longer your own. These are horrible people to live with. If they were good roommates, would they walk in when you were reading the paper and rip it out of your hands? Would they scream and interrupt every time you try to kiss your wife? Would they stand up in the middle of a restaurant, throw food, knock over glasses, and cry until you have to beg for the check? No.

People don't tell you these things when you're deciding to have children. They show you pictures of cute babies in Halloween costumes, and clean-faced toddlers sleeping like angels on unruffled beds. They tell you that having children is the best thing they ever did, and that they can't imagine a life without them. These are tales from prisoners who forgot what life was like on the outside.

Another thing they don't tell you is that you will never sleep again. We all know sleep is rare when they're babies, but the truth is you won't sleep for the rest of your life. You think you're sleeping, you lie down like you're sleeping, you close your eyes like you're sleeping, but you're listening for trouble twenty-four hours a day. You are now a volunteer fireman for the rest of your life.

In the middle of the night, my little one threw up off the top bunk bed. All I had to hear was a single chirp. She didn't even know what was happening yet, and I was up from my bed, running like a marine in his underwear, grabbing anything that looked like a bucket. I tried for a pillow, then the cat, and ended up using my hands.

I did more chores that night, in ten minutes, than I did in four years of college. Bagging stuff up, carrying bodies, doing laundry, it's like I worked for FEMA in the middle of the night. She came down the hallway with stuff still in her hair. "Am I okay?" "No. Go stand in the tub. Get her out of here. She smells," I said, while gagging.

When it was all over and she was back in her bed sleeping, I took a shower, lay back down, and stared at the ceiling for hours, listening for the next sound of trouble, until it was time to make breakfast.

Please keep in mind, this wasn't some ludicrous tale from one awful night. This is what life with children is like. If you go into a home where children live, there isn't a single room that hasn't been thrown up on, peed on, bled on, pooped on, spit on, or cried on. It's a war zone.

But these are also the same rooms where first steps were

taken. Where they said "Mama" for the first time. Where good report cards were hung and where "Happy Birthday" was sung. These are the rooms with pencil marks on the doorways keeping track of how much they grew. Where dinners were held and everyone laughed so hard they couldn't eat. These are the rooms that, without these little people, would be difficult to call "home."

And that's how they get you.

welcome to plain pasta, can i take your order?

Feeding children is the worst. Not the starving ones in distant lands—they'd at least be appreciative—I'm talking about the ones who live in my house. It should be joyful and gratifying when you make something and feed the ones you love. But when the ones you love are under three feet tall, that is seldom the case. Feeding your own children is more nerve-racking than cooking for a cranky *New York Times* food critic who just had his car towed.

My kids don't like anything. They eyeball their plates like an agent on *CSI* looking for DNA. They see a speck of pepper and they completely shut down.

"What's that green thing?"

"Why is this different?"

"Mom doesn't make it like this."

"Is this a different kind of veggie burger?"

"I'd like to see the chef. Oh, you are the chef? Well, you're fired."

I honestly don't get it. When I was a kid I was a garbage can. I ate stuff the dog passed up. If I didn't recognize a food, I didn't even ask what it was, I just figured it out by eating it.

Liking it was beside the point. I hated brussels sprouts but that didn't stop me from eating them. I crammed them into my mouth, washed them down with some milk, and moved on. I was just happy that somebody gave me some food. Maybe that's why at eight years old I was the same size I am today.

My sisters were more picky. They would poke at the green beans and make horrified faces at whatever was underneath the brownish gravy. I remember them having classic old-school standoffs with my parents where they had to finish their dinner or they wouldn't get to leave. They usually got out of it by feeding the dog and me under the table.

I think we give our children too many choices. I don't remember eating out, or ordering in, or stopping off at the Starbucks drive-thru for a cotton candy latte. We played all day, got so hungry we couldn't take it, then ran home and ate what they gave us.

My kids walk into the house like it's Applebee's and immediately ask to hear about the specials. If they don't like the answer they let me know about it. And if they hear that their sister *does* like it, they immediately don't.

I tried for years to make them happy. Maybe they'll like this? Maybe they'll like that? But nothing worked. When I failed to come up with anything, I thought, *Maybe if we just don't feed them, they'll get so hungry they'll have to eat what we give them.* This could have worked, but my wife doesn't like starving our own children as much as I do.

When I was living in New York, I met parents who were proud that they finally got their children to eat by giving them sushi. How is this a good thing? So in order to get the kids to eat you have to whip out the credit card and act like you're taking a big client out on a business dinner at Sushi Dan?

After all these years I just gave up. No more trying to get them to like fish or looking for recipe ideas on the internet and talking to other parents. I'm done trying. From now on all they get is plain pasta. It's the only meal that never disappoints. It's nothing but starchy noodles with virtually no vitamins or minerals, but they eat it every time and, at this point, that's all I can ask for.

If I had the money and the energy and knew anything about business I would open a restaurant and call it Plain Pasta. Do you realize how popular this would be? Families would be dying to get a table at Plain Pasta. Anyone with a child would be making reservations months in advance, planning their birthday parties and ordering take-out.

How happy would kids be in a place where plain pasta was the only item? It's tailor-made for them. Their parents can't suggest that they try the scallops or eat a vegetable because there aren't any. There isn't even a pepper shaker in the place.

The parents will be ecstatic too, because they wouldn't have to worry about what to feed them. They could skip ordering altogether. Walk in, sit down, and *whammo!*, a big bowl of plain pasta is slammed down before them like it's feeding time at the zoo.

By the way, this is not affiliated with my other popular restaurant, Chicken Fingers. That place is a little more down and dirty. There are no utensils at Chicken Fingers. There aren't even napkins. You pick up your chicken fingers with your hands, out of a metal bucket, dip them one of our twelve dipping sauces, and wipe off your hands on your jeans.

There are chairs for the adults, but not at the tables. The parents sit in lounge chairs around the outskirts of the room, drinking beer and wine, while the kids run around the place

grabbing chicken fingers, eating what they want, and throwing the rest at their friends.

Oh, what sweet irony it would be if I were to become a
millionaire from these two restaurants! For years my kids
don't eat a thing I make and suddenly, here I am feeding the
children of the world. A celebrity chef from just two dishes.

It could happen.

the kid with the googly eye

One of the most basic instincts we have as parents is to protect our children from danger. From the moment the baby is born, our minds begin showing us short films of all the horrible things that can go wrong. While we are able to put those plastic things in the wall sockets and fences around the swimming pool, the one thing we can't prevent is the ridicule from other children.

No one in the history of mankind has gone through life without having their flaws pointed out and mocked by other people, especially young people. Nobody's perfect and if you think you are, spend an afternoon with a group of third graders and you'll soon find out why you're actually pretty gross.

My memories of being a small child are spotty, at best. I see flashes of being outside, something with a sprinkler, my mom in the kitchen, a rat stuck in the garage, pretty much stuff like that. What I don't recall is being unhappy or ever looking in a mirror. However, from the moment I started school, my memories are crystal clear, because that's where, for the first time, I learned everything that was wrong with me.

I was slightly larger than most of the other kids who showed up at kindergarten, and this slight variation in size was mulled over by the other children, discussed, and presented back to me as "Hey, Fatso!"

That was it. I was the fat kid. Fatso, Fatty, Tub-o-lard, Lard Ass, and Tommy Salami were just some of the clever nicknames my classmates came up with. It didn't matter that I wasn't even that fat; that's how they saw it, and that's what they went with.

I'll admit, there were a couple years when I was on the chubby side. I distinctly remember being in the third grade, at a new school, and being stuck on the rope in gym class. While the lighter kids climbed right up to the ceiling in a matter of seconds, I pulled my fat ass halfway up, got tired, and just held on and cried. Eventually someone came and got me. This did nothing to change my nicknames, and to this day I still think I'm fat. And have a fear of ropes.

I really do.

That's the real reason why we want to protect our children. Because we know this stuff is powerful. It sticks. If it didn't stick and wasn't so effective, there is no way that I would remember all the kids in my class so perfectly and what was wrong with them.

There was Flintstone. His real name was Joe, but he happened to have a large, blockish head, with dark black hair and a simian forehead, just like Fred Flintstone. I'm sure his parents thought he was adorable, his grandparents likely thought he was an angel. They probably called him "Cute as a button," but we called him Fred Flintstone. Right to his big, square face.

Over the years, and it truly was years, his name was modified simply to Flintstone. He signed my high school yearbook that way.

I can't believe it's over. Have a great summer! —Flintstone.

The hard part about Joe's flaw is that he was really stuck with it. You can change your shirt or buy longer pants, but he couldn't change the fact that his head was the same shape as one of the most popular TV stars of the day, who also happened to be a cartoon caveman. I'm sure he's in a business meeting somewhere right now, trying to impress his colleagues, looking pretty much like everybody else, but any time one of his ideas falls flat, I bet a little voice inside his head yells, "Way to go, Flintstone!"

Diana was a smart girl who had a lot going for her, as well as two large buckteeth that stuck out of her face, even when her mouth was closed. I just looked up the origin of "buckteeth," as it sounds kind of cruel to be an acceptable description of this condition, and the definition confirms this fact. The term comes from buck (deer) and teeth (teeth). Her classmates weren't thinking of a deer when they saw Diana smile, which she stopped doing altogether because of the mockery. If the kids saw a deer they would have called her Bambi, but instead they called her Bugs, after another popular cartoon character of the day, Bugs Bunny.

Easter season was particularly horrible for Diana. Kids would literally hop up and down around her, like rabbits, and sing "Here comes Peter Cottontail, hoppin' down the bunny trail." In case she didn't get the point, they would lean in, make carrot-chewing sounds, and wait for a response.

She never gave them one. She probably turned out to be a model.

Brenton was Chinese. In those days that was enough. There weren't a whole bunch of Chinese kids in New Jersey, so if you were from a different culture and had different-shaped eyes, that was enough.

A lot of kids had their clothes made fun of, which is really unfair because a kid doesn't shop for her own clothes and is really at the mercy of her parents' taste and how much money they have. When someone mocked your sneakers you knew they weren't the cooler, more expensive ones and your only recourse was to look for someone who had even worse ones than you.

Then there was John. He was extremely short and really little. He was so little that his hands looked like cat paws. They used to call him a midget, a shrimp, or a leprechaun. He didn't like that and tried to fight back, but he couldn't do much because he was so damn little.

Another drawback about being such a small kid was that other kids tried to stuff you into things. It was like a game of "Will He Fit?" Poor little John was stuffed into boxes, gym bags, lockers, cubbyholes, milk cartons, cat carriers, and anything that looked like it might carry fruit. It got to the point that he would try to head off the embarrassment by seeing something, like a grocery bag, and simply climb into it himself.

Being too tall was another problem. It must have been strange for Chris to be only eleven years old and be called a giant by his classmates. His burden was that he was the victim of one of the lamest and most repeated bad jokes of all time. "How's the weather up there?" He must have wanted to pound them with his colossal fists.

And then there was Kevin. Kevin was in real trouble because he had several unique things about him and had to carry the burden of fending off attacks on multiple fronts. To start with, Kevin had a big round face like a snowman, made even bigger by his giant glasses that looked like two round, fun-house mirrors, creating the effect that his eyeballs were spinning around in different directions.

The other thing that stood out about Kevin was that, regardless of the season, time of day, or level of activity, he sweat like a leaky faucet. He would show up, first thing in the morning, already streaming sweat, as if he'd just made a quick stop at the sauna or took a dip in the lake before he came to class. I doubt this was a medical condition as much as it was just pure nerves. He would anxiously sit at his desk, looking through those goggles, with his one giant, google-y eye, just waiting for someone to make a crack about his enormous head.

I'm sure in his home, on the mantle, there was a photo of little Kevin's giant coconut in a nice frame. One of those early photos taken at the mall, posed against a fake tree, with a little smile on his chubby face. I'm sure he was truly happy back then, in his sailor outfit and shiny shoes, before he even knew what a school was. Can you imagine the shock his parents must have felt when they first found out that the other children called him Blockhead?

That's why it's better that a parent doesn't hear those things. You are powerless to stop these little hooligans, so don't ask questions unless your kid comes home with smashed glasses demanding that the house go up for sale.

And although I realize that I can't prevent my children from being surrounded by mean kids with nasty things to say, I know that I don't have anything to worry about. Because naturally, my kids are perfect.

your baby doesn't want to go anywhere with you

First off, your baby really wants to thank you for the onesie. It fits great and it's really warm. They love it. And they're sorry for throwing up on your shoulder the other night. They don't know what happened. It just came out of nowhere. They were just as shocked as you were.

They love you and are grateful for everything you do, but they would greatly appreciate it if you'd stop taking them with you *everywhere you go*. They want to stay home. They're a baby.

A baby doesn't want tapas, or to stand in line at Bed Bath & Beyond, or sit in the stroller while you blab on and on in a crowded coffee shop. They're a baby. If you take them to these horrible adult places, they're going to cry. That's what babies do.

Babies want to be home. Home is built for babies. The temperature is always perfect, just warm enough that they can roll around in nothing more than a diaper, with Cheerios stuck to their stomachs. Some they'll eat, some they'll stick in their belly button for later. They look around, see their toys and blankets, and they smile that toothless smile of happiness.

And then, out of nowhere, you grab them, rip the remote out of their hands, turn them upside down, and stick them in layer after layer of clothes. You don't ask if they want to go, you don't ask if they're busy, you don't even tell them where you're headed, but they know if it's a place that requires pants, it can't be good.

It makes sense that you like going out, you know where you're going, have people you want to see, and like dressing up. Babies don't have appointments. Babies don't have to run errands. Babies aren't bored. Babies don't even talk. The outside world isn't made for babies; leave them at home.

From where they're sitting, the world is an ugly and aggressive place. It's all knees, asses, and animals. They try to Zen out and gaze at the horizon and suddenly a German shepherd sticks his wet nose in their face. Imagine if every time you went out a giant beast licked your face and stole your snacks. You'd want to stay at home too.

And where are you taking these poor babies? Your friend's weird studio apartment filled with incense and cats? Furniture shopping? An airplane? These are all terrible places for a baby. Truth be told, they don't even like the park. Maybe later, when they can really walk and run, but not now. It's just another uncomfortable place where they lose their balance, fall to the ground, and get licked by more hounds.

I can't believe where some people bring their babies. I was at a Jay-Z concert and the couple next to me had their baby with them. I was horrified. I wanted to run up to the stage and ask Jay-Z to lower the volume a little before the baby's ears exploded. My ears were ringing for hours when I got home, so I'm sure that baby's deaf.

And why are all these babies being dragged to sporting

events? It seems like every other night ESPN shows some dad catching a foul ball with his bare hand while he holds his helpless infant in the other. Everyone applauds that this dad was able to make the catch with a baby attached to his hip when they should be using the clip as evidence for child services and arrest this guy.

Why would you bring a baby out to a baseball game filled with flying bats, balls, and beers? Especially when it's televised and broadcast to your home, right next to your baby's crib filled with stuffed animals? And why isn't it your first instinct to cover the baby with your body when a line drive rockets toward you at 150 mph? And why does Major League Baseball sit these maniacs in the front row of the upper deck? Is this the new baby zone? Is baseball so boring that you need to entertain the fans between innings by dangling children over the guardrail?

Let them stay home and, while you're at it, you stay home too. A baby is a built-in excuse. A baby can help you get out of anything.

"Hey, you guys want to come to a karaoke costume party?"

"Sorry. We'd love to, but we have to stay home with the baby."

I've skipped fishing trips, lame dinners, WNBA games, kids' birthday parties, old people's birthday parties, canoe trips, one-man shows, amusement parks, Cirque du Soleil, christenings, wedding showers, engagement parties, weddings, nephews' T-ball games, back-to-school nights, elementary school band concerts, dance recitals, poetry readings, you name it. All because of the baby. And, as happy as I was, I know for a fact that my baby was even happier.

So please, if you love your baby, let them stay home. You

have a whole life ahead of you when the two of you can run around to dumb places. Before you know it, the two of you will be standing in line at the port-o-potty during a Foo Fighters concert. But for the next year or so, enjoy yourself at home and give your baby a taste of the good life. Warm up a bottle, turn up the thermostat, and leave them naked on the couch.

boys stink

Boys stink. Girls don't stink. They may smell at times, but mostly like coconuts, strawberries, jasmine, and love. Boys smell like meat. Really old meat that has turned brown and has worms in it and that most people would throw away, unless of course that person is a twelve-year-old boy, in which case he would eat it. If girls are flowers, then boys are the worm-infested soil, filled with manure that covers their roots.

Now, I know we could get caught up in a gender-bending, anti-generality discussion and all come up with an example of a boy who smells like a flower and a girl who smells like an old taco, but I'll leave that to you and your book club. I'm sticking with the boys I have known throughout my life, who reeked like a bad egg on a hot day. I am one of those boys.

Another one of these stinkers is my nephew Sam who once came to spend the night in my New York apartment, wearing sneakers that were so old they smelled like they had been passed down from his great-great-grandfather who never washed his feet. Before he even rang the doorbell, the smell came roaring under the door as if it was a planned attack. It didn't make sense that this cute eight-year-old boy was emitting the smells of a rotting fish carcass, but the minute he came inside we knew it was him.

After I resuscitated my wife, we made him take off his shoes and leave them out on the steps. Within minutes the superintendent knocked on our door and asked if we knew anything about chemical weapons and if it was possible that we were being invaded.

It seems impossible that his parents were able to sit in the car with him during the hour-long drive from New Jersey (there's a smelly New Jersey joke in there somewhere), but Sam was one of three boys who all smelled equally as bad, and the parents, like workers on a pig farm, just didn't notice it anymore.

There was my friend Doug, who wore the same Bob Seger T-shirt for an entire summer. This would've been bad enough if he'd worked in an air-conditioned office, but we are talking about a kid running and playing in the woods for two months. At first he smelled a little dirty, then rancid, and then it broke through to the other side and was just him. We got used to it, the same way that you come to expect a bucket of wet leaves to smell like a bucket of wet leaves. When his mother realized that she hadn't seen any laundry from him for weeks, she had his brothers hold him down while she squirted him with a hose.

Why do we smell like dirty ashtrays filled with moldy cheese? Because boys, and men, for that matter, actually enjoy horrible-smelling things. Anchovies, scotch, and cigars are not merely tolerated by men, but embraced and used as a type of cologne. It doesn't matter that women are repulsed by these smells, we just can't get enough.

Girls may like the smell of cut grass, but we like the smell of manure. When it's the time of year to spread some old cow dung on the lawn and start seeding the grass, my daughters stay inside for days at a time. I sneak outside, lie on my back, and make dirt angels.

We like the smell of destruction. Burned tires, burning leaves, melting plastics, basically anything on fire. We like gas fumes, oil-filled garages, and the undersides of toenails.

Even our activities reek. We like to fish, cut up bait, slit the stomachs of deer wide open and pull out the liver. These smells don't bother us; they make us feel like we belong. A horse stall may be disgusting, but it makes us a lot more comfortable than the perfume department at Nordstrom. We are talking about a gender that farts in bed and tries to keep the smell in by holding down the covers.

Boys don't even realize that they smell until someone from the outside, probably a girl, gets a whiff and starts yelling through her tears that you're foul. For a guy, that's like being told that you have a mouth and eyes.

"Yeah, of course I stink, I just don't know why you're pointing it out."

One of the bravest of all public servants has to be the teacher of sixth-grade boys. How they can do their job without wearing a gas mask just doesn't make sense to me. These are boys who are at their peak of stench-hood and avoid bathing at all costs. They don't make windows big enough to release all the horrid, prepubescent odors wafting around those desks. It's like trying to teach geometry in a monkey cage filled with spoiled sour cream.

I hated showering so much at that age, that I would try to fool my mother by sitting in the bathroom with the water running. I had an intricate system of getting the soap wet, dampening the towels, even sprinkling water on the floor. I thought if I could get to my room and put on my pajamas quickly enough, she'd never know, not realizing that I still smelled like dog sweat. It would have been so much easier to simply bathe.

It's almost worse when boys get a little older and start to care more about what the girls think of them and they try to do something about it. You would think that discovering deodorant would be a good thing, but he's just going to abuse it. It's like giving a Porsche to a drunk.

I couldn't believe this stuff had been around all these years.

"Why didn't someone give this to me before?" I asked. "I just have to rub it on? Amazing. I'll never have to shower again!"

Eventually we get it together and go on dates and interviews, smelling the way the rest of the world wants us to. But, make no mistake, we're only doing this for you. We'd be okay smelling like a bag of old bananas. It actually sounds kind of cool.

how to yell at
your children

I don't have a bad temper. I've never been so overcome with rage that I've thrown a glass against a wall. I don't slam doors or peel out of my driveway with Black Sabbath pumping through the speakers.

Most of the time I am calm, cool, and collected, preferring not to let life's little annoyances get me down. But every once in a while, I do get mad, because the people and animals I live with are disobedient maniacs and never do as they're told!

They say you should never act out in anger. That is true, but if you're reading this I feel like I don't really have to say it. If you picked up this book I assume you have a good enough sense of humor that you aren't one of those people who actually knocks others around. We have more fun than that.

But we all lose it from time to time. We're only human and every so often our blood pressure is going to spike into the red zone. But while we are all prone to fits of anger, I would make the argument that we should try and be a little more creative about it. Try to avoid the overused, hacky phrases that parents have used for way too long. They're lame, archaic, and only give the children more reason to not take you seriously.

"Why doesn't anyone listen?" This was my father's favorite. As if the only thing a kid had to do was hear an order from him, one time, and we'd leap into action. Hearing him wasn't the problem, agreeing with his dumb rules was. When he declared "No TV on a school night," we heard him perfectly, but we thought he was completely insane. There are a lot of school nights, and a lot of great shows, so, No; let's pretend we didn't hear that one.

When he would catch us in the act, he really thought it was a communication problem. When he caught us a second and third time, he thought we must not have been that bright, which was fine because the dumb kids always get to watch TV.

"Am I invisible?" My mother, like a lot of moms, would often ask this question. But mine asked it so much I started to believe she was sincerely asking. She truly felt there was a very good chance that she was walking around the house and could see all of us, but that we looked right through her.

She would see a sock on the floor or shoes by the door and yell out, "I asked you to pick these up! Am I invisible?" If we didn't answer right away she would wave her hands around, touch her head, and look in the mirror to make sure she was still there.

"When I was your age . . ." This is one of the worst. As if the kids didn't already think you were older than dirt, now you give them proof.

"When I was your age, we didn't have smartphones. We had one landline, attached to the wall by a cord. If you wanted to talk to your friend you had to stand in the kitchen while the whole family sat at the table, stared at you, and listened."

Although they don't say it aloud, what the kids are really thinking at this point is, *How are you still alive?*

"Who lives like this?!" My friend Karen told me that whenever her father would see a mess in the house or dirty dishes in the sink, he would cry out, "Who lives like this?!"

As if it wasn't his home at all, but some sort of a fraternity house at a clown college that he accidentally stumbled into while looking for a screwdriver.

Here are some other gems:

"How many times do I have to say it?" Endlessly, until your grave.

"I'm going to count to three. One, two . . ." This one is tricky because up until about the seventh grade it actually works. From that point on you get to "three" a lot.

"You're killing your mother!" This one has been used for decades and has the opposite effect of what you want. You're trying to create overwhelming guilt in the child, but instead you appeal to this tiny, adorable creature's dark side and give them a taste of power they never thought they had.

"Honestly? Seriously? Are you kidding me?" Yes, yes, and no.

It should be noted that coming up with original and effective ways to yell at your children is not easy. The world is filled with dumb statements that parents make when the words just can't keep up with their anger. Your voice says authority but your words say you're an idiot.

"If you don't start listening, I swear I will put you in the pantry, where the cereal goes. For a whole bunch of days."

"Go ahead, see what happens. You'll end up with a pizza in your backpack, mister!"

"If you don't pick up these shoes, you won't have any more shoes, because I will give them to the children who really need feet . . . and shoes."

Unless you're going for laughs, these kind of threats are pretty useless. But, then again, getting them to laugh might actually be the better way to go.

morning people

I used to love sleeping. I mean, really love it. Sleeping until ten was an early day. Sleeping until eleven was expected. Noon was the norm. The only reason I would get up earlier than that was for something horrible like a doctor's appointment or catching an early flight, which was a guarantee that I'd be dizzy and nauseous for the rest of the day. I got up once to see the sunrise, and what made that special was knowing that I would never see it again.

I liked sleep so much that I only took jobs that guaranteed that I didn't have to wake up early. This kept me dirt poor for years but it also kept me in bed.

Those days are over. I literally haven't slept past 8 A.M. in over fourteen years. It's ruined. My life is ruined. We had children and made a family and the price I have to pay is that I will never sleep again.

I had heard about "morning people" in the same way one hears about an unusual ancient tribe living in the Amazon. They seemed strange and unknowable and I had no idea what they did. I pictured them walking around on wet streets that some old lady sprayed with a hose, before the rest of us woke up. They had their coffee, shared a muffin with a bird, and read the entire *New York Times,* crossword puzzle included, right before they went to the market. Morning people are always scurrying off to the market with their pushcarts filled with recycled bags, to pick up what's in season. Only morning people would do that. What's in season?! What does that even mean? Everything is in season. Welcome to the future, when we get apples all year round and order them on our phones while we're still in bed.

Morning people are the worst.

I never bothered to even meet those people. What was the point? If I suggested that we go to dinner and a movie, they'd say no, because they had to be in bed by nine so they could get up early. Getting up early was a choice, and they were choosing the morning over the night. Who does that? What kind of person skips out on communal, music-filled, starlit nights so they can sit by themselves in the early morning, crunching quietly on a bowl of wretched bran flakes?

The sad answer to that question is I do.

I always said that you'd have to kill me before I'd get up early, and that's exactly what happened. I had children and they showed up and killed that part of me. The part of me that enjoyed doing adult things after sundown. Like, movies that start after ten, stopping at a diner at midnight, and sleeping until the rest of the world was at work. I enjoyed going out and drinking without worrying that a child might appear at the foot of my bed at 4 A.M. with the news that they just threw up.

Of course, I knew that no one sleeps when they have a baby. It's an obvious fact that once you live with a small, helpless person there will be many sleepless nights. I would've thought, however, that after a couple years of this, things would return to normal and we'd all sleep in and meet up at brunch.

Well, here's a secret that no one tells you: You will never sleep again!

Ever.

First off, there's school. That horrible, relentless schedule that tortured you your entire childhood comes back and drags you down all over again. Their schedule is your schedule, and suddenly you're up with the sun, day after day, week after relentless week. You start to really need Christmas vacation, every Jewish holiday, and, despite all the new evidence that he wasn't a great guy, you beg to keep Columbus Day because maybe you'll have a chance to sleep in until seven.

Then there's gymnastics, ballet lessons, and soccer. Never-ending, year-round, weekends included, soccer. I didn't realize that every activity your kid joins, you join too. You think your kids just head off to practice on their own and you show up for a game or two? No way. You have to get there hours before it starts because you've been picked to set up the nets, and next week you have to bring orange slices, and stop at Costco to pick up eleven hundred juice boxes by eight A.M.

On the rare days that there isn't school or activities, there's still breakfast, and a dog that needs walking, and a cat that just puked, and a kid who just peed on the cable box. Family life is an endless series of events that you have to participate in, and you can't do it while you sleep.

The worst part is that now, even when I'm alone, I still can't sleep! They broke me. They changed me. I am a morning person. I am wiping tears off my keyboard as I write this.

I'm now one of those people who is constantly doing sleep

math while they're out. "If I fall asleep right now I'll get five hours of sleep," I'll mutter at a party, to no one but myself.

I know exactly how much sleep I'm going to get because it's always subtracted by the time that I get up every day. Six. Six o'clock in the godforsaken morning! I'll be at a concert with a friend, the band is halfway through their first set, and I'll hear myself say out loud, "I'm going to go. If I fell asleep right now I'd get only seven hours of sleep. And I still have to find my car and get home."

I don't stick around to see the look of puzzled disappointment on their face.

Six A.M. That's four hours before ten. Four hours! Of what? Good times? Hanging out with my friends? Telling stories? Laughing? No! I can't call anyone because no one I like is up yet and they won't be up for hours.

I can't even go to stores. The mall isn't open until ten. I know this because I have actually sat in my car in the parking lot waiting for it to open. Me, alongside a bunch of old people in sweatbands and running shoes who are going to walk the mall for fitness so they can live a little longer, be strong enough to get up early again tomorrow, and walk around the Chick-Fil-A some more.

Sometimes I'll wander into a diner. You know who you see at the diner in the early-morning hours? A bunch of other depressed people who have been broken by children who needed to get to school on time, and screamed until they were fed. Those children are off, out into the world, living lives of their own, as their parents mindlessly stir their coffee, trying to remember what happened to the last eighteen years.

This is how I know it's over. The other day I actually said to my wife, "I like getting up early. Six to six-thirty is my time. Before the kids get up and the whole day starts. I really look forward to it."

She just stared at me, as if she was looking for some hint in my eyes that this was the same man she had married. But I'm not.

I'm a morning person now.

in defense of
family vacations

A vacation with your family can be a tough, disorienting, sticky, exhausting, irritating, soul-crushing rip-off, but you have to do it.

This is not your blissful romantic getaway. This is a vacation that is made for the family, not a rational adult person. You will stand in line for things you do not like, pay for things you do not want, and order food for people who do not eat. You will go to theme parks and eat things on sticks. You will wear a bathing suit in a public place for an entire day and you will swim in hotel pools, next to people you would normally cross the street to avoid.

You will play in the sand, sleep in the woods, and sit on benches. You will carry strollers up escalators, cat carriers through security, and everyone's luggage. You will pull muscles, rip shirts, and pop handfuls of Advil like popcorn.

But go you must.

This is your only real chance to get to know these people. At home you don't really hang out. Everyone has their schedules and their work to do, coming and going like bees in and out of the hive. Then you wake up that first morning together in a hotel room and look at each other. You really look at them all and realize that these people you live with are pretty weird.

"So, this is my family," you say to yourself. "How did we all get here? Look what they're doing. The little one doesn't look like any of us."

As weird as it is for you, it's even more bizarre for the children. Sure, kids live with their parents, but to be this close, for this long, gets a little peculiar. I remember sitting on the hotel bed in the morning, waiting for my father to come out of the bathroom.

I would think, *What is he doing in there? What's taking him so long? And what are those noises?* It sounded like a bear rummaging through a dumpster filled with balloons.

Eventually he'd come out and announce with a snicker, "I wouldn't go in there if I were you."

But there was nowhere else to go. I would stand in the bathroom in pools of water, with my eyes watering, trying to brush my teeth and hold my breath at the same time, thinking, *My God, how does my mother share a bathroom with this guy every day?*

Watching your parents get dressed is weird too. It's like being backstage at a play for the first time. It's one thing to see everybody onstage in their complete costumes, but it's pretty bizarre to see your mom hopping across the floor in her underwear, trying to get her foot into the leg of her jeans, or lying on her back trying to zip them up around her belly.

Once you're through all of that and you get out of the room, the rest of the hotel is great. There's something about that hotel smell, the welcoming lobby, and the other families walking around. It's so great to be out of your house exploring somewhere new that might even have a game room.

I couldn't get over that one. A game room? Are you kidding me? This didn't exist in other places. There was no other room in the adult-run world that was designated just for games. And I'm not talking Monopoly or checkers, I'm talking real games, like Asteroids, Pac-Man, and Donkey Kong.

The only thing that was more exciting than a game room was the pool. Kids enter the lobby of a hotel sniffing for chlorine like a pig after truffles.

"I think they have a pool. Do they have a pool? They have a pool? An indoor pool? Did he say an indoor pool? Oh my God, can we live here forever?"

That's all you need to make your family happy. These don't need to be expensive excursions to the other side of the world. If you want a vacation, just load them into the car, stock up on gas-station snacks, and find a hotel with a working ice machine.

This doesn't mean that the experience will be pure joy, because it won't. The chances of everyone in the family being in a good mood at the same time are pretty rare and every age comes with its own bad attitude.

Of course the smaller they are, the more work you'll have to do. First, you have to plan the whole thing because they don't know where anything is, they think New York and L.A. are right next to each other. You'll also have to pay for everything because they have no money or skills of any kind. For years you'll also have to carry everything that they own. Literally, carry everything in a pile on your back, and they climb on top of that pile, like a small Peruvian lady, as you walk through the airport like a mule. Like a human mule, with canteens hitting your legs and flies in your eyes.

Have you ever seen a donkey with flies in his eyes and

think, *Why doesn't he get those flies out of his eyes?* Now I know. I have seen a donkey's soul. He doesn't care about the flies in his eyes. He's secretly hoping the flies eat through his eye and devour the part of his brain that feels and remembers.

Then the kids get a little older and start wheeling their bags around on their own. This is a huge moment. The first time my children glided through the airport ahead of me with their own luggage I almost started to cry. Keep in mind this doesn't mean they know anything about packing. Don't be surprised when you get to the hotel and the only thing they have in their bag is a Curious George doll and some magnets.

"Really? Two weeks' vacation and you thought that was going to do it? Well, I hope you like that bathing suit because you're going to be wearing it a lot."

They're thinking, *That's all I'll need, pal, see you at the pool.*

When they get even older, every idea you have for a fun day is boring, the worst, or "really?" But it is your job, your duty as a parent, to make plans and force your family to participate. The more angry they get, the better. Do it all: a tram ride up the side of a mountain, a cowgirl museum with a stagecoach exhibit, or a half-mile walk to stare at an aircraft carrier. You have to do the things that they would never do on their own because these are the things they will remember. A teenager is never going to ask to take a ferry ride to look at the tulips in the botanical gardens. You should do that for them.

My new thing is hikes. We are going on a lot of hikes. Wherever we are, whatever we are doing, I'll add, "And then we can go on a hike."

They groan, scream, and say mean things about me and it fills me with joy. And I only get happier when we hit the trail and I look back at these noodle-legged kids, trekking along, thinking I'm an idiot.

This is the stuff that will stick with them and, whether they are aware of it or not, will add to their experiences and their personalities, turning them into good citizens of the world. At the very least it will give them something to post on Instagram.

The family vacation truly is a must. When you return as a family, back from the day, be sure to reward them with a swim in the indoor pool, some lame hotel pizza, and give them one last image that will stay in their mental scrapbook forever: you snoring away in your underwear.

the happiest place on earth?

And now a word about Disney World/Land or that Euro-version Thing. I was going to include this in the family vacation chapter, but it's too big and important to be lumped in with all that. This is different.

They call it the happiest place on earth. And I have to ask you, dear reader, "For whom?"

I like the idea that Mr. Disney wanted to create a place where families could go and their children could let their imaginations wander and everyone would feel safe in this horrible world. What he couldn't foresee, when he was designing the place in the 1950s, was the type of people it was going to attract in the United States of America, in 2017.

They didn't make these kinds of people back then. There weren't dinosaur-size people marching around the park with their elephant children attached to their tails, roaming through the parks, pushing the biggest strollers I have ever seen. I had no idea that John Deere made strollers.

There are some people who come to the park who don't have any children at all, but they want to be a princess. They want to dress up like Cinderella, but they don't make a Cinderella dress for someone forty-five years old, six five, and three fifty. They never had a meeting at Mouse Headquarters where Goofy stood up and said, "Let's make more of those."

Does that stop these giant princesses? No, it does not. They buy that dress, stuff everything they've got into it and not all of it fits. There's a lot of extra hanging over the sides. This doesn't bother them; they have their wand in one hand and their autograph book in the other, and they chase down the poor girl playing Snow White, and they're happy there.

There are some people who have a baby just so they can go to Disney. They come straight from the maternity ward, with the kid still covered in goo, and the umbilical cord waving behind in the parking lot. Now, that's fine, I'm not going to judge you. I don't know what kind of emotional hole you're trying to fill, but what's not cool is breastfeeding in line at the Minnie Mouse house in front of my hungry children. Now my kids are eyeballing my wife and I have a problem I have to deal with.

I really didn't think we were going to go. I thought we'd avoid the seductive allure of Disney. But once you make your own people, the ads just find you. Every time you open the laptop, turn on the TV, glance at your phone, there's Disney selling you familial perfection. The mom is beautiful, the dad is handsome, and they're looking back at the kids, who are holding Mickey's hand, saying, "Thanks, Mom and Dad, for not being stupid and poor."

I'll admit it. I wanted to be that family. I wanted us to be perfect. But we were not that family. We weren't close to perfect. We were hot, sticky, fighting, and cursing in front of the children.

"This whole thing is your damn fault."

"My fault? If your mother didn't raise you like an animal we would have gotten on the road earlier. . . ."

And yet the kids don't hear us because they were slapping each other in the face. And we hadn't even parked yet. We're still in the van and we're angry because we didn't get to park in Mickey and Minnie parking, they sent us to the ass end of Chip 'n' Dale parking. That's another three tram rides and an extra thirty minutes that we didn't plan for.

I know it's a cliché, but when you finally get to the front gate, you open your wallet and they take everything you've got. Every dollar, every coin, credit cards, gym memberships, pictures of your family. That mouse rapes you at the turnstile in front of your family. You're seeing the college fund go up in smoke, but you do your best to keep a smile on your face because you don't want to ruin the Happiest Place on Earth.

Once you get inside, everyone is excited; they're ready for the good time and it comes to a screeching halt. It's just line after line. I thought I was going to beat it. I had the app on my phone, I was ready for them. But you can't beat Disney.

I thought, *Let's go on the Peter Pan ride, that's a lame ride from 1912; look, the line only goes back and forth two times.*

Yeah, up top, but then it snakes around in the basement for a couple miles, shoots out the back, and goes around the Matterhorn five times. All this and it's a bad ride. There are old cardboard cutouts, blinking Christmas lights that don't work anymore, and the voices are all jumbled.

Tinker Bell sounds like an old, bar-soaked truck driver. "Come with me, I'm Tinker Bell. Let's get some Jack Daniel's and shoot some cans."

This ordeal took two and a half hours. Was it worth it? No. What would be worth it? Nothing. I could get to the end of that line, there could be naked supermodels with bags of money and all-you-can-eat nachos, and I'd still be angry.

Here's the one important thing I learned. If you have to go to Disney—and if you make your own people, eventually you'll have to go—you only want to go once. So you have to go big. Blow it out. Make it all about the children. Give them your money.

"Here's $300 cash, kids. It's your day, spend it the way you want to spend it."

Halfway up Main Street they'll be broke, because they're little, stupid, and gullible. Without thinking, they'll buy a bunch of blinking stuff that won't work by the time they get outside. Now they're sitting in the gutter of Main Street like little Disney hobos, with broken toys, just yelling at the characters, "Get over here, duck. I got nothing left. Come over here and shake your ass."

You also have to let them eat whatever they want. Make sure it has artificial flavor, artificial color, and a ton of sugar.

"You don't even have to wear sunblock, kids. You don't want it, I don't want to put it on you, don't wear it. I bet you don't even burn at Disney."

But they do burn, especially when they're little. They turn purple and they start to blister. Now they're burned, crashing on sugar, with broken toys and this is when you walk them. Walk the hell out of them.

Let them be in charge of the map. "Here you go, kids. Lead the way. Anywhere you want to go. Oh, you want to go from the *Cars* ride to It's a Small World? Sure, they're twenty miles apart, let's start walking."

By the time midnight rolls around, they're exhausted,

confused, and have only been on two rides. We'll never go back again. When my kids see that mouse on TV, they shake like they went to war with it.

The best part is, your children will learn a valuable lesson: the happiest place on earth is home.

no fighting before coffee

I wake up every morning and try to greet the day with a good attitude. I'm not jumping up and dancing around at the foot of my bed—my ankles won't allow it—but I am quietly thinking to myself, *Let's make the best of it.*

And then I open my bedroom door and enter what can only be described as the chaos of an emergency room on New Year's Eve. People are running, cursing, and screaming in complete panic. Kids are being yelled at for being too slow, there's a lot of crying, and we are always running out of time.

This is a school morning; my wife is going nuts and I haven't had a sip of coffee.

No one is eating right, eating fast enough, or cleaning up after they're eating. They haven't combed their hair the right way, they've looked at their phone too many times, and she doesn't like their attitude.

"Don't you roll your eyes at me."

I know mornings are tough and getting kids out the door is next to impossible, but I don't see how this strategy of yelling at everyone is helpful. Imagine a captain of a rowing team who sits at the front of the boat with the little megaphone and instead of yelling, "stroke, stroke!" they just scream abuse at the rowers.

"You always use too much syrup. Why are you always late? Did you pick up your socks? I'm going to take away your phone. Don't use so much butter. Why are you wearing that?"

Not only would that team lose, but the rowers would jump overboard and start swimming for shore.

Why all the panic? This isn't life or death. If you mess up in the emergency room someone could die. What happens if we're five minutes late for school? Nothing. Not a damn thing. The kid will need a note? Well, I can write a note. I can write notes all day long.

We're late. Yours truly, Mr. Papa. You want another note? Let me get some paper. Here you go: *Sorry we're late again. If it looks like my daughter was crying on her way to school, it's because she was. Not a big deal; my wife just said something about her hair. Have a great day. Mr. Papa.*

It's not a big deal, but my wife thinks it is. She thinks if they're late, it will go on their record and force them out of honors classes and into community college, where they'll end up marrying some guy who stands outside the 7-Eleven and vapes for a living.

When I was a kid I used to watch cartoons, and there was always the father at the breakfast table hiding behind his newspaper. I remember thinking that this dad was rude and mean and didn't care about his family. Now, as a father, when I sit at the table hiding behind the paper, I realize that old-cartoon Dad was just hiding in his foxhole, trying not to get his head blown off.

When my wife reads this, which she will, she'll say, "Oh please, what do you know? I do everything. If I don't do it, who will?"

How about the kids? If they don't, they'll go hungry and get in trouble for being late and the next day they'll hustle up. What's the big deal? That's what happens when my wife goes out of town. The girls know if they want something done they've got to do it themselves, because that man over there with his belly sticking out of his shirt (that's me) isn't worth asking.

They know if I make their lunch they'll get to school and find what is technically a sandwich, but not the kind Mom makes. Mine have too much mayonnaise, or not enough mustard, or the wrong amount of cheese. The bread is weird, the way it was cut is even weirder, and why did he wrap it in newspaper?

The same can be said about breakfast, their hair, and the laundry. They know if they want it done right they have to do it themselves. Just like real people. We come into the kitchen in the morning like coworkers starting our day. We say quiet good mornings, make a corny joke, and go about our business. And if someone is late, so be it. Try harder tomorrow.

Not every move they make in the sixth grade will determine whether or not your child ends up living under a freeway overpass. The idea that these kids can make such big mistakes, at this age, as to put their future in jeopardy is insane. They aren't capable of screwing up that much. That won't happen until they're older and start mixing vodka martinis with credit cards.

Another reality that we have to consider is just how long we are actually going to live together. They won't be living here forever, so why all the tension? Let's stop all the yelling and make the experience as enjoyable as we can. Truth be told, life will do a better job of disciplining them than we can. Trust me, if they show up late to school, dressed as Batman, with no pants on, they're going to hear about it. We discipline them enough; let's at least have a nice morning.

They won't be perfect, no one is. So if they're pouring chocolate syrup on their oatmeal, and spilling it on their sequined cape, that's okay. The day is just getting started. Just sip your coffee and let them be. And if they do something that really makes you mad, save it up and let them have it at dinner.

least popular baby names

Hank
Rocky
Squirrel
Moo Shu Pork
Sluggo
Swizzle Hips
Donald Trump
Rat-Face McGee
Cruella
Marge

school sucks!

I don't want to go to back-to-school night, I don't wanna go! The whole time all I'm thinking is, *Didn't I do this already? A long time ago? Why am I back in these classrooms sitting in these tiny chairs having to listen to a teacher all over again?*

I find myself staring at the clock the same way I did as a child, just praying for it to be over.

But as happens every year, I'm quickly reminded that these new teachers are pretty great. They are bright and enthusiastic and actually seem like they want to be there. There are a couple stinkers, for sure, but grading on a curve, teachers today are light-years ahead of the musty, alcoholic child haters that we had.

The only requirement to become a teacher at my school was that you had to come with your own unique odor. All my teachers smelled like some combination of Vicks VapoRub, tuna fish, and cigarettes. They would all huddle outside, smoking with their tar-stained fingers, glaring with resentment at the children. They saw us as running around without a care in the world, and thought it was their job to change all that.

I had a science teacher, Mr. Ulak, whom I'm convinced was

part monitor lizard. He had leathery, scaly skin that looked like he had been raised somewhere on the outskirts of the sun. Kids used to say that he was doing an experiment in his basement, and as he was flipping the switch on his giant science machine, a lizard happened by and changed his DNA.

He was squirrelly and anxious and flew into fits of rage. This was a common trait among all my teachers. I never understood why they became teachers, when just being in the room with children made them so angry. That's like a taxi driver who loses it whenever he's in traffic. Maybe you're in the wrong line of work. Send out your résumé and take some meetings.

Mr. Ulak wore awful, muted polyester suits, that awful fabric created during the great plastic rush of the early 1960s when plastic was being put in everything. It looked like clothing but had a little extra shine to it and didn't breathe at all, which made Mr. Ulak's choice of wearing polyester suits with a turtleneck shirt underneath, all while chain-smoking, just more confirmation that he was indeed an actual lizard.

The problem with an angry science teacher is that a science lab is already a dangerous place. It's filled with gases, compounds, beakers, and fire. And if you don't like children to begin with, and you think they're idiots, you certainly aren't going to have much patience watching them try to dissect a frog with a scalpel. He would get angry and start throwing all the implements around like a pissed-off surgeon on his last day of work.

This was an era when the teachers were allowed to be mean to the students. They would throw things at us, yell at us, say very hurtful things. It wasn't a big deal to us, we just thought that was how the world worked. It's not like today, when we expect everyone to act in a civilized manner and respect each other. If Donald Trump had come around back then, no one would've been offended, they would've made him the gym coach.

But while the teachers were mean, the students could be even meaner. Not to everyone, but if you were one of the teachers who made our life hell, we were going to do so in return.

We had a tiny, little teacher named Mr. Mano. He stood about five feet tall, which was a little shorter than most of his students at the time. To make himself taller he wore high-heeled boots and combed his dark, greasy hair into a tall rooster-type pompadour. Even though he added inches, both down low and up high, he still got lost in a busy hallway filled with children. This made him very angry.

He wore impeccable suits with a little vest and little buttons on it as if to say, *We might be the same size, but at least I dress like an adult.* And if you didn't get the message that he was in charge, he would get your attention by throwing something at your head.

He threw everything at us: erasers, pens, pencils, notebooks, textbooks, copy paper, rulers, paper clips—these were not school supplies to him; they were weapons, school-funded projectiles to be flung at students for even the smallest infractions.

He used us for target practice. Stare out the window, an eraser would bounce off your head. Caught whispering to your neighbor, a ruler would whiz past your cheek.

"What's that in your mouth, gum? In my class? Better duck because here comes a stapler."

He was little but he seemed to have superhuman strength, like one of those carpenter ants that can lift twelve times its weight. We actually saw him do this when he picked up an entire desk and threw it into the hallway with Jason Paul still sitting in it.

Now, before you feel bad for us, you have to realize we weren't going to sit back and take it. No way. He might have been little, and he had authority, but we could fight back with a child's greatest weapon: truthful ridicule. And the truth was, Mr. Mano was the smallest man outside of a circus we had ever seen.

We took this creep down with the power of song. I'm not sure what budding musician came up with it. It might have been a collaborative effort from several brilliantly evil minds, but a song was sung, recorded, and broadcast through the PA system for the entire school to enjoy. We were as coordinated and devious as delinquent Navy SEALs.

This song drove him crazy. Literally. I still remember the exact words. It was short but effective.

He got his feet cut off in Viet-nam.
Can't even reach the inter-com.
(Pause)
(Screaming) Mano! Mano!

The Mano part was screamed as loud as we could. It drove him crazy. Picture that angry little man making his way through the crowded hallways when he hears someone singing this song. *"He got his feet cut off in Viet-nam. . . ."*

He tries to get up on the tippy-toes of his high-heeled boots and strain his little neck, but he can't see anything but kids' belt buckles.

"Can't even reach the inter-com . . ."

Now he's jumping up, trying to get a look.

"Mano! Mano!"

The whole place laughed, but if you were on your way to his class you'd better put on your safety goggles, because stuff was flying your way.

We had an art teacher who looked like "The Most Interesting Man in the World." Part wolf man, part international lover, he would come up behind the girls, in class, and massage their shoulders and rub their hair. In class! We couldn't claim sexual assault because that didn't exist back then. It was just that creepy teacher who touched all the girls.

I had a shell-shocked history teacher who smoked so many cigarettes that smoke continued to pour out of his nose and ears throughout the class.

There were a few good ones. They were mostly women, of course, who didn't completely lose their minds, probably because they had never been to war like many of the men.

The teacher who I went to war with was the music teacher named Mr. Lerner. He was tall and doughy, with a wiry mustache, and he was the angriest of all the teachers. He was belittling, always telling us that if things had worked out differently with his band there was no way he would be stuck teaching us music. From his chubby, milky appearance it must have been a polka band, in which case this job was a promotion.

As a result, a lot of kids screwed around in his class, but for some reason I got under his skin unlike anyone else. I'll admit that I wasn't the best, but the fury that I conjured up in that man was insane.

One day, on a dare, I tossed a pen that landed on a giant kettledrum while he was teaching. I scared him, which is never a great thing to do to a bully. Of course I should have been disciplined, maybe sent to the principal's office, but he was so angry that he took me into the hall and pinned me by my neck against the lockers.

He growled in my face, "One day you're going to realize there's more to life than f*ing and football." Exact words (except the long version, which I won't write) that my seventh-grade teacher felt okay about screaming in my face.

Now, I already knew there was more to life than that. I played football and it was a lot of fun but that was just something to do after school. And f*ing? I was thirteen years old! I was quite a ways from doing anything close to that, so I didn't really understand his point. I do remember thinking, *Well, if it's even half as much fun as playing football, it should be pretty great.*

This man shoved me into the metal lockers, spit this sage advice at me, but trapped himself. There was no way he could send me to the principal's office, not after assaulting a child. He was stuck. Stuck with me returning to his class with a pocketful of pens and a roomful of drums.

It's really amazing I learned anything at all. I think about Lerner, Ulak, and all the other wackos we battled every day, especially as I sit at back-to-school night, looking at my daughter's teacher. He's wearing a Winnie the Pooh tie, earnestly telling us something about providing extra counseling so that every student can excel.

As nice as he is, I have to say, when I sit in this tiny chair my defenses are up. I have a hard time concentrating on what he's saying because to me, school still sucks and I'm too busy trying to come up with a song about him.

family life

A family is in a constant state of "we." There is no "me" in family. There is an "i," but that's been crowded about by the f, a, m, l, and y. Y is the worst, totally annoying and never stops asking for money.

Being single is like running a small shop. We need small shops; small shops are great. If you don't want the hassle of going to the mall and fighting for parking, you go to the small shop. One guy, sitting behind the counter, mints at the register, great.

Family life is like running a corporation. There are elevators, boardrooms, and never-ending meetings. Everyone walks around in a constant state of panic, trying to survive cutthroat politics, power struggles, and hostile takeovers.

Unlike working in the simple solitude of a small shop, when you are in a family you are never alone. Even when I travel thousands of miles away from my home to do some show, my family is always there, on my mind, on my phone, and popping up on my screens.

"How did she do on the test? Is the dog still licking the

refrigerator? Can the plumber come next week and get that doll head out of the toilet?"

I have friends who don't have families who ask themselves very different questions. "Which show should I binge watch for the next six hours? Should I go to the gym in the morning or at midnight? Should I just stay in bed today?"

These are questions that I never ask myself because that would be focusing on myself and my self is no longer relevant. That's why parents are always so goofy-looking—they're too busy thinking about everybody else. When you see a dad walking down the street with mismatched socks and his fly down, he's probably just trying to figure out how to fix the garbage disposal or pay for college. (I swear to you, I just noticed my fly was down.)

It's funny to think that there was a time when I thought that having a family was a choice. It wasn't a choice. You choose how you want your steak, whether you sit on the aisle or window. Having a family was just nature taking its course. There was the illusion that perhaps I could have gone in another direction, but truly I could not.

The ghosts of my ancestors were all around me, waiting for me to make more people, and that's what a family is, a factory for new people. Big ones, little ones, funny, and funky. They are constantly calling, texting, and inviting you to birthday parties. You will never be alone again.

That's fine with me. I'm not really at my best when I'm alone. If I was, I wouldn't have spent my entire career in front of crowds. But then again, at my shows the audience sits quietly, listens to me, and applauds. My family has never done that.

someone threw up there

There are very few things in life that can't be cleaned up. I'm not talking about relationships or money problems or fights with your dry cleaner. I'm talking about physical messes that take place in the home for a whole host of disgusting reasons.

A home is a lot like a city street. While you're standing on the corner waiting for the walk sign, daydreaming about your shopping list with your face in the sun, you have no idea that just last night, in that same spot, a man was stabbed to death for his wallet.

This was a spot of complete panic with police cars, emergency workers, reporters, and power washers, and it all went away without a trace. All it took was a little soap and water and it's as good as new. Just like that time the cat threw up on your counter.

We had a crime scene in our apartment in New York caused by a second-grader with a weak stomach. She came over for a playdate and she just didn't look right. She'd come over before and while she never looked that great, on this day she was really teetering. I asked my wife if this child normally stares into space, puffing her cheeks like a hamster, but she thought I was just being funny. Within minutes, the kid went from white, to green, to vomit machine.

If children ever cleaned anything, or saw the house as something other than their own private bouncy castle, perhaps they would be more selective about where they throw up. This girl certainly wasn't. She stood motionless right in the hallway, opened her mouth, and as everything that she'd eaten since kindergarten flew out of her, she decided to take a stroll toward the living room, to spread it all out.

It was so horrible that I seriously thought about taking out a book of matches and lighting the place on fire rather than trying to clean it up. At those moments it just seems impossible that the smell, the stains, and the memories will ever go away. How could I possibly invite guests into our home and ask them to sit on this sofa and eat bean dip when I saw, firsthand, the horrendous wrongdoing that occurred here?

The things that a dog can do in your home is enough to make you reconsider having an animal within one hundred feet of your property, let alone allowing them to sleep in your den. I know there are disputes about their ability, but I swear that I have watched my dog put her ass on my pillow, look at me, and laugh.

I was watching TV and my cat dropped his ass on the floor, lifted his back legs, and, with his front paws, started pulling himself across the carpet. Straight at me, six feet across, didn't break eye contact the entire time. He just stared me down, as if to say, *That's right, my ass and your carpet. What of it? What are you going to do about it? Go in my box? I don't think so.*

Two days later my kids are lying in that same spot, rolling around and reading a book. Home, sweet home.

How about the gifts that the cat brings in? They say these are gifts of love, which makes me feel that our cat has the biggest heart in the animal kingdom. He's given us dead mice delivered in two pieces, injured mice trying to make a run for it with one leg, and punctured birds released in our bed. My daughter once woke up in the middle of the night with a mouse rustling around *in her hair*! My wife woke up to a dead hummingbird on her chest. My other daughter received a live rat in her bathroom who threw in the added bonus of peeing in her shower cap. Luckily she noticed it just as she was about to put it on her head. We've had birds with one wing, birds with no legs, birds who just gave up, laid on their backs, and begged us to kill them.

How about rugs filled with dog pee? Windowsills covered in cat vomit. Shoes filled with cat vomit. Blankets filled with cat vomit. My cat throws up so often he must think it's the top line in his job description. "If you're looking for someone to throw up, rub their ass on things, and throw up again, I'm your cat."

As I describe all this, you may think that we live in a canvas lean-to in the Adirondack Mountains, using muddy leaves for blankets, but we actually live in a house in Southern California with walls and everything.

There are many theories as to what stopped the five-year drought in California, but the real reason the rain and mudslides came was because God noticed that we got a puppy. He wanted to learn just how much we loved this animal by seeing if we would be tempted to kill her when she ran through the house covered in mud. I came real close.

But let's not just pile on the animals with their baseball-size brains. There are plenty of human beings who do more than their share of nasty things in the home and should know better. Myself included. I once tried to trim my back hair with a pair of left-handed kid scissors, turning the shower into a dog-grooming van. To this day, I still find random, runaway hairs hiding near the soap dish.

Should I mention what our houseguests have done? My father has done so much damage to my home that I actually looked into homeowner's insurance for the guest bathroom. My brother-in-law enjoys buying expensive red wine almost as much as he enjoys spilling that same red wine on my carpet.

And what about where we keep the food? We have a drawer next to the sink where we put onions and potatoes that we never cook. One day I heard a creak and saw a potato opening the drawer by itself using the vines that grew out of its face. We had only lived in the house for two years, but this potato must have been living in that drawer for half a century or more.

Have you ever seen an onion that is so old that it turns black and starts to eat itself? I have. Have you ever seen brussels sprouts transform into green-and-yellow jelly soup that somehow manages to not leak through the plastic vegetable bag, in the vegetable bin where all good vegetables go to die? I have.

The bombs that have gone off in our kitchen make a war zone seem mild. Glass jars of tomato sauce, smashed. Whole bags of flour, exploded. A jar of honey turned upside down and dripped down along the sides of the cabinets. I once put hand soap in the dishwasher, because my brain likes to make up its own rules, and by the time I came back inside, the entire kitchen was filled with soapsuds like a scene out of *Willy Wonka & the Chocolate Factory*.

At least that was soap. In all these situations, soap is your friend. What an amazing invention that was. The cavemen would have moved along a lot faster and cut down on years of domestic abuse if only they'd had a bottle of Palmolive.

My wife, in her noble pursuit of keeping everyone in the nest safe and healthy, has experimented from time to time with all-natural cleaners. You've seen these products if you've ever gone to a farmers market or got lost in a Whole Foods or spent the night at your hippie sister-in-law's place. They are made of things found in nature, like rosemary and sage and sugar and spice. But the problem with these products is that in times of crisis we aren't looking to be one with nature, we are looking to clean nature up and get it out of our house. Forget saving the environment, we need Mr. Clean. We want to see that bald bastard in his tight shirt and his earring. I don't know if he's gay or straight or a pirate, I just want him looking at me from under the sink. "Yeah, I might kill your cat, but I'll leave this place smelling like lemons."

Ajax is another good product in a time of tragedy. This stuff is so badass that they don't even put a lid on it. They know if you're reaching for Ajax you've done, or seen, something terrible and can't be bothered with unscrewing, uncapping, or opening anything. They just put a sticker over the holes and stand ready with their industrial-strength cleaning crystals to restore your life to normal.

Whatever product you use, pick your favorite, put on some rubber gloves, and get to work, because trying to live a perfectly sterile life is impossible. It really doesn't matter what part of the planet you get your mail delivered to, this is just what happens when you live with other human beings. I guarantee you that right now someone is picking their nose and wiping it on the arm of your couch. And tomorrow you'll be having a drink there, as if nothing ever happened.

worst family vacation spots

Walmart
Jake's Plumbing Supply
Carl's House of Nuts
The L.A. River
Fresno
Vladimir Putin's House of Fun
Death Valley
Man-eating Monkey Island
Linoleum City
Disney World
Hormel Meat Processing Plant
LaGuardia Airport

nuttier than a fruitcake

There are many reasons for your family to get together: reunions. Birthdays. Weddings. Funerals. Taco Night. These events can be fun and relaxed or end with people screaming with their shirts off on the front lawn.

When there are old people around, these get-togethers can seem like they're playing on a loop, because they act the same way every time. They use the same lines and get in the same fights, as if they're characters in a never-ending Broadway play. Any time I saw my grandparents they started playing their roles right on cue.

"Your grandmother is nuttier than a fruitcake rolling around the loony bin, ooh boy!"

That was my grandfather's line while in the middle of one of his classic anti-family rants. I remember sitting in the passenger seat of his yellow Honda Civic, watching him chain-smoke cigarettes and spit profanities about our family, all while speeding through town under yet another overcast New Jersey sky.

"And your uncle is a little light in the loafers, ooh boy. He really loves watching that figure skating. I had to get the hell out of there. I couldn't breathe," he said as he puffed another cigarette.

This happened at every family gathering, which happened about once a week, not because it was anyone's favorite thing to do, it was just what we did. My grandfather enjoyed it the least, becoming more and more annoyed until he was on the verge of exploding, at which point he would come up with some excuse to run to the store, tell me to get my coat, and we'd escape.

I liked that he picked me and not one of the adults and definitely not one of my two sisters. What would he talk about with them anyway? Ballet? Flowers? No, he asked me because I was a man. A ten-year-old man. He knew we could talk baseball and guy stuff and, more than that, I wouldn't run back and tell everyone what he had said about them during our ride. My sisters would totally tell.

"Your father is a piece of work, ooh boy. Who does he think he is, sitting on my side of the couch? He thinks he's a regular king of England that one, driving around in a Buick and a ten-dollar shirt," he said as he ran another red light.

Sure, he was taking the stuffing out of my own father, but he was good with a phrase and the only adult who ever asked me if I wanted a smoke. I liked that, even though I never accepted. The only thing I was hooked on at the time were Pixy Stix and Fritos. My grandfather, however, inhaled cigarettes like they were keeping him alive, which for many years they did. Until they didn't. He constantly had smoke pouring out of him like he was a house on fire. He smoked like they did back when health wasn't even a word. Back when Lucky Strike was considered a breath mint.

I understood why he ran away from his own home like

this every week. It was a suffocating, small house in Clifton, New Jersey, about five miles outside of the city. The type of neighborhood that wasn't quite industrial but wasn't quite hospitable, either. There was a factory nearby that constantly pumped sweet-sour smoke into the air that smelled like a mix of baby food and burning tires. Whenever I asked my grandmother about it she'd wave it away and tell us not to worry.

"I kind of like it, don't you? It smells like bubble gum." That was enough for me. What kid is going to argue with a mystery factory that filled the sky with candy?

The house was so small that everyone looked bigger when they were in it. That's part of why I liked it. I was adult-size there. The door handles were at my level, I didn't have to reach up on my toes to get a glass from the cabinet, and the tiny bathroom made me feel like I had already gone through puberty. The only downside was that it made the adults seem larger too, as they drank wine out of thimble-size glasses, bumping into furniture like drunk giants trapped in a dollhouse.

Even their dog was small. His name was Pip-Squeak, Pip for short. He was a miniature poodle–Chihuahua–chipmunk mix. He was the smallest and ugliest dog I had ever seen. There was a time when I wasn't sure he was a dog. He had strange little ears and his legs were all different lengths, which caused him to wiggle and roll across the floor like he was always sneaking up on something. The biggest thing on his body was his eyes but even those weren't right. Not only did they go off in different directions but they didn't even start off in the right place. One was spinning off to the right and the other seemed to be doubling as a nose.

The TV room was the size of a walk-in closet. The only place to sit was a plaid corduroy couch wedged in the corner.

My father, who is a large, broad-shouldered man in normal spaces, would sit on this couch wedged between my grandfather and my uncle Richard like they were fighting over the last seat on a crowded subway car.

The TV was rolled into the room on a shaky metal stand with four white plastic wheels that were never headed in the same direction. This was back when no one really knew how to make things and the things they did make didn't work so well. Everything was made of metal: wastebaskets, lawn chairs, beds—all metal. Metal springs stuck out of mattresses and couch cushions. Children fought for their lives on metal playgrounds. Even aspirin came in tiny metal boxes. And, in my grandparents' house, there was a metal antenna that stuck out of the TV that was used to capture shows from out of the sky as they were flown through the air to your home.

Imagine that.

I was forced to sit on the floor because it was the only remaining space and the men liked to put their feet on me like a human ottoman, when they weren't using me as their remote control and antenna adjuster. These three giant men, squeezed together on the couch like martini olives, would bark orders at me to change channels and hold the antenna at different angles, sometimes during the entire game, because for some reason the signal was stronger when it passed through my body.

On this particular day, my grandfather was quickly losing patience because the only program we could get was men's figure skating, which made him very uncomfortable, especially while snuggled up with these two couch mates. Then my grandmother, who I called Nana, came in and really set him off.

To be clear, I loved this woman. She dressed in bright colors with flowered patterns that most people only had on their wallpaper or shower curtains. She had flowers on her shoes that matched the flowers on her headband, that matched the flowers on her dress and purse.

I was her first grandchild and clearly her favorite. No one even came close. She called me "The Miracle" and, although my sisters hated to hear that, I had no reason to doubt her. She was the greatest. But that was my relationship with her.

Her relationship with my grandfather was a different story.

They met as teenagers when she was in love with Frank Sinatra. My grandfather had Sinatra-type hair, which apparently was good enough, as my grandmother didn't seem to notice that his face was closer to that of a basset hound than Ol' Blue Eyes. They fell in love, got married, gave birth to my mother and my uncle, and lived happily ever after. Or at least for a couple years, until the stress came in.

No one called it "stress" in those days, they just called it "life" and it was hard and you didn't complain, you just did your best to deal with it. There were no massage parlors or therapists or friends who wanted to hear your bellyaching. You quietly got stressed, got angry, and eventually exploded. Men punched each other in the face on a regular basis. My grandfather wasn't violent and he wasn't a drinker, he was just a confused man who wandered onto the deck of a ship called "Fatherhood" in the middle of a storm and suddenly everyone was calling him Captain. But he didn't know a single thing about sailing, so he just held on to the mast and screamed his head off.

Yelling in my family didn't mean you were angry, you were just communicating in a timely fashion. Today, the neighbors would be concerned and call child services or marital services or whatever kind of services that stop people from screaming in the middle of a Sunday afternoon, but yelling, to us, was normal.

We knew the screaming was about to start the minute we heard Nana marching in her daisy shoes down the short hallway to the TV room.

"How much time is left in this stupid game?"

"Two minutes," my grandfather would yell back.

"Oh, sure. I'll believe that when monkeys fly."

"Well, they must fly because there are two minutes left. Ooh boy!" he yelled louder.

"Don't you 'Ooh boy' me. And, Tommy, don't stand so close to the TV, your eyes will turn to jelly."

"Leave the kid alone."

And this was when my grandfather would turn to me.

"Goddamn it, get your coat, Tommy, it's time to go to the store!"

Relieved that I could finally let go of the antenna, I ran and grabbed my jacket and we went out into the candy-coated air and drove away. Sometimes we'd really go to the store, but most of the time we just drove around and he'd yell and smoke until he calmed down. I always thought it was funny that no one ever questioned us when we returned without any groceries, but they were probably just relieved to have him out of the house for a while.

His peaceful nicotine state didn't last long when we returned because then it was time for dinner. The time when everyone was forced to sit at the table. Together. My parents, my sisters, cousins, my aunt and uncle, and a random neighbor or two, maybe their kids and my great-grandmother, who lived in the attic.

That's right. I had a great-grandmother who lived in the

attic. We called her "Oma." And it was my job to go up there and get her. People don't live in attics. Ghosts live in attics. Scary things that hide from the living stay in the attic. Seriously, who lives in the attic?! And why was it my job to go get her?

Fifty steps straight up, each step creaking with doom and dead things and demon spirits. I'd climb each death-defying step, gripping the handrail until I got to the top, where I'd knock on the door, slowly open it like a coffin lid, and there she was.

And the fear went away.

She was a smart, funny, eighty-year-old German immigrant who would simply rather stay up there in her room than have to deal with my grandmother. I could coax her down by making her laugh, which she always did, but when she smiled things would get scary again because she had no teeth. Many times they were left on the table, still biting on a cracker.

Ooh boy.

I'd get her teeth in and lead her down the stairs.

"Everybody, sit down and eat!" yelled my grandmother.

There we were, multiple generations of stressed-out, overworked, funny-looking people with flowered headbands, crooked teeth, and tar-stained fingers, screaming and eating while Pip-Squeak licked at our ankles with a tongue that stuck out of where normally an ear would go.

What more could you ask for?

no phones at the tablay

"Put down your phone. Get off your phone. Leave your phone. No phone at the table. Are you on your phone? What did I say about the phone? How long have you been on your phone? No phone in your bedroom. No phone during homework. Put down the damn phone!"

All we talk about is the phone. We talk so much about the phone, and how much the kids are on it, and who they are texting, and what material are they looking at, and what time of day they start, and how long they're on it, and how late they posted on Snapchat, and how many minutes they've used, that I can't figure out what parents used to fight with their kids about.

Without the phones it seems like there wouldn't be a care in the world. Cleaning the dishes, walking the dog, picking up laundry? That sounds like a dream.

It's like a strange science fiction story. Alien devices sneak into our children's bedrooms, sit on their nightstands, and slowly eat their brains. The device then tells the children to carry it with them everywhere they go, follow its orders, and ignore their parents'.

When my daughter was little she made a sign that read, NO PHONES AT THE TABLAY. It was cute and to the point, and obviously written by someone who didn't have a phone yet. We hung it up by the kitchen table and used the phrase for years. The whole family would laugh and put their phones away. All that changed when she got her first device.

Look, I can't blame them for their addiction, I'm hooked too. These devices are powerful. Anyone who has seen *The Matrix* or read about the singularity—when man and computer merge as one—knows what's coming. Reality is being transformed and eventually human beings will be as important as double-A batteries. In the not-too-distant future we will look back from our slave quarters and remember that it all started when we were playing *Candy Crush* on our smartphones.

These really aren't phones, they're supercomputers. The entire knowledge of the world is literally in your pocket. When you reach in and touch it with your thumb you are one click away from being transported to another world, a new state of consciousness, or every season of *Full House*. It's so vast that our brains sometimes can't figure out where to begin, so we just robotically click on the dumb news site we always go to and spend several hours scanning through Instagram.

At its best it's truly beautiful—being able to meet people around the globe, walk through every museum, listen to all the music ever made. But you can also be led, or choose to go, to the very worst places and see things that you really shouldn't.

Most likely our children reside somewhere in between, in an endless barrage of entertainment. We like to be entertained. It's fun, amusing, and addicting. If I were a kid and I had all my favorite cartoons sitting in my pocket, I would've acted the same way my children are.

"You want me to look out the window during this three-hour drive and listen to you and Mom argue about your drinking? Okay, let me just turn off *E.T.* so I can focus."

But I'm not a kid, I'm a grown-up, and it's up to me to do the impossible and try to control what the kids do on their phones. There's no way. I've taken their phone away and noticed they were still able to post on Instagram. My daughter could be a mile underground, with nothing but a block of wood, and she would find a way to Snapchat.

Parents trying to police kids on their smartphones is like a substitute teacher trying to catch the cool kids vaping. By the time I enforce something, they've already found a way around it. I told them that since I paid for the phone, the phone is mine and I'm just letting them use it. This means that I can look through the phones whenever I want.

I knew this wasn't going to work because they didn't put up a fight. At all. They didn't even flinch, they just happily handed over their phones. Of course they had nothing to fear, because their phones were completely scrubbed. No text history, no browsing history, nothing. Clean. Like a politician who knows the FBI is close to exposing their secret love affair.

The only time I did see something on my daughter's phone I felt like a completely overbearing jerk.

"What's this, a text from a boy? Here we go, let's look at this."

Here's the text exchange:

Daughter: Hi.

Boy: Hi.

Are you excited for Halloween?

Totally.

Me. Too.

What's your favorite candy? I like KitKats.

I like Skittles.

Lol. Smiley face.

Dancing girl. Dancing girl.

Confetti.

Gotta go. Homework time.

I felt like an idiot. That was some real hard-core, under-cover surveillance work.

But for all the high-tech problems that this presents, the solution is actually very simple; just be a mean, boring, lame parent. That's it. How easy is that? They already think you're mean, boring, and lame most of the time, so just do it. Be the mom who's no fun. Be a buzzkill. Be the person they complain to their friends about because they couldn't text for two hours.

Let them be bored. Let them be with their own thoughts. Let them know that this is what a life is, not a celebrity's Instagram posts about their asses. Let them be present in whatever mundane activity is happening in the home. Make them look a family member in the eye and listen to their never-ending stories. Make them look out the window when you are driving along a beautiful tree-lined road or a dilapidated town or a vast prairie of nothingness.

It sounds lame. It is. So do it.

Tell them, "No phones at the tablay, with your family or by yourself. No earbuds when it's time to talk during this long-ass ride, no phone in the restaurant, no phone in your room, no phone, period."

Because we are the only people on the planet who are going to show them that there are boundaries. That there are limits to what they should be doing. We are the drain catch at the bottom of the cultural shower and it is our job to stop them from falling into the sewer.

You don't have to ruin everything for them. You can let them enjoy their lives, but childhood is not a free pass.

And here's the thing that makes it even easier: You don't have to tell them why you're doing this. Don't try to make it poignant, or sell them on the message. Teenagers will not understand that having a conversation with Grandma and smelling her cooking will nourish their soul and last a lifetime. They'll get that down the line.

So your job is easy. Just be boring. Just be lame. That's it.

And when they angrily storm out of the house, whip out your phone, get on Facebook, and tell me all about it.

stay out of the
emergency room

Here's a good rule to live by: Stay out of the emergency room. If you go about every day trying to avoid that place, the rest of your life will be lived the right way. If you're in there sitting on a table with a form in your hand, something went really wrong.

"Don's in the emergency room and they're trying to sew his head back on. He was opening a can of tuna and did something wrong with a fork. And you should see the guy next to him."

Even jail isn't as bad as the emergency room. If you go to jail, sure, you're in trouble, but chances are you're not bleeding. Maybe a little from being punched in your lip, but at least you'll get to lay down, make a phone call, and meet some new people.

You don't want to meet anyone in the emergency room because they're a mess too. If you're battling explosive food poisoning and a guy walks in with a chainsaw sticking out of his chin, chances are, you're not exchanging numbers.

I was taken to the emergency room only once as a child. I was five years old and I was running around barefoot in the backyard while my parents were having a barbecue. I ran up to my father, who was sitting in a chair drinking a beer, and suddenly pain shot through my foot and straight up my leg.

I jumped up and screamed, which was pretty typical behavior for me, and my father told me to calm down, which was pretty typical behavior for him. When I couldn't stop, he looked down, saw a bumblebee attacking my middle toe, and swatted it with his brown beer bottle. It was a Michelob, with a tan label that was torn on one side. We remember the strangest details of a tragedy.

He told me not to cry as he carried me into the house, sat me on the bathroom counter, and stuck my foot in the sink to relieve the pain. He went out to do something, probably get another beer, as I sat there quietly crying and looking at my foot that kept getting bigger. When he returned, moments later, his eyes popped out of his head from fear because, apparently, unbeknownst to any of us, I was allergic to bees and was swelling up like a bag of microwave popcorn.

He grabbed me and ran out of the house, into the car, and off to the emergency room. I didn't know what was happening. I was too small to look in the mirror or even know what questions to ask. When you're a kid you really have no choice but to go with the flow, trust that the big people know what they're doing, and try not to cry.

I remember thinking that it was the only room I had ever been in that had curtains for walls. It felt like I was watching a strange play starring giant doctors and nurses who were trying to figure out why I had become a bee. Obviously my brain wasn't getting much oxygen at the time.

My father is very clear on the actual facts. Apparently it was an actual life-or-death event. He said it was one of the scariest moments in his life, especially after they gave me a shot and it didn't work. I just kept swelling up like a blood-filled tick and started struggling to breathe. It was only after a second shot that the drugs took effect, my air tubes cleared, and my father grabbed me and ran out of there.

That's the thing about the emergency room, you need it to save your life but you want out as soon as possible. We went back to the house where my father rejoined the barbecue, drank a ton of beer, and I started a new life being terrified of bees.

I had to take my daughter to a New York emergency room when she did a flip off our bed and landed headfirst on the dresser. In the city you don't call 911 for something like that, you just get a cab and head to the hospital. I remember thinking how bizarre it was that no one gave me a second look as I was hailing a taxi while holding a bleeding toddler. It takes a lot to move people in New York.

I had a pocketful of jelly beans that I kept feeding her to keep her calm. I, on the other hand, like my father, was freaking out. Anyone with a heart condition would do well to not have children. When the smallest of things can attack you with fear, something like a run to the hospital with your child can truly give you a heart attack. I'm really surprised that she wasn't happily picking out a lollipop while they carted me off to the ICU.

The worst part was having to hold her down as the doctor stitched up her head. She kept crying and yelling that she couldn't take it anymore. She'd never used that phrase before and it just took my legs out. I just kept telling the doctor that I couldn't take it either. When we finally got home she walked into the apartment and started playing. I sat in an empty bathtub and drank a bottle of scotch.

Just like my bee tragedy, her trip to the emergency room was far worse on her father than on her. I asked her recently if she remembered anything about this event. All she can recall is something about a fun taxi ride with a bunch of jelly beans.

tell me that story again

If you spend time with anyone older than you in your family they will undoubtedly tell you stories from their lives. You will hear these stories over and over again, at holiday gatherings, barbecues, and birthday parties. They will be told by people who often have food in their mouths and alcohol on their breath, completely unaware that they've told you this tale a thousand times before. But these are the only stories they've got, because although a lot happens in a life, there are only a couple tales worth retelling.

You may be bored with these stories. You may wish that the old-timer would gently fall asleep in their chair and never wake again, but this impulse is wrong. These stories must be told, again and again, and you must listen to them, every time. They are as much your stories as theirs, and they give context to your life and an understanding, no matter how goofy, of your family's place in the world.

Now, keep in mind that these tales are passed down through the years in a messy game of telephone and rely on the memories of old people, so there's bound to be a lot of mistakes and whatever they can't remember, they'll just make up. But that's what history is: a bunch of stories, filled with exaggerations, passed down through the years by unreliable sources.

Jesus walked on water? Okay, if you say so. Lincoln studied by candlelight in his remote cabin in the woods? Says who, the owl hanging out nearby? And why is that a good story to pass down, anyway? To show he was studious? I think it shows that he was a weirdo.

I always picture Abe sitting there in the middle of the woods, parents sleeping two feet away, and this maniac is burning candle after candle, reading the same book over and over again. It sounds like Jack Nicholson in *The Shining*. His parents must have peeked out from under the covers as this giant grasshopper was muttering to himself and thought, *This kid's a loser.*

But this story sticks because it speaks to where he came from. We all want to know how we got here, especially as we look around the table at our relatives, who don't seem like they'd be able to find the front door of a Walmart, let alone devise our creation.

Most family history starts with the love story. My children lean in a little closer when we start telling them how we met. Everyone wants to know, "Was it destiny? Was it a mistake? Somehow we think this might have been a mistake."

I enjoy a good reluctant love story. It's always funnier when you hear that Grandma took one look at Grandpa and almost threw up.

"He came over and tried to talk to me and I thought, *Oh my God, get this guy away from me!*"

Everybody laughs at the picture of Grandpa being rejected. But it also makes the story more believable. And it adds a little "what if" to our lives. What if he had stopped trying? What if someone better had come along? What if he hadn't been able to get Grandma drunk? None of us would be here!

According to family legend, when my grandmother first saw my grandfather he was sitting on a bench in Jersey City with a bad sinus condition. He was leaning back, with his runny nose in the sun, when my grandmother came along with some of her friends and saw this dreamboat with his nose toward the sky and thought, *Get a load of this weirdo.*

That's all I know. They may have told me more, but that image is so strong and bizarre that anything that comes after it seems inconsequential. Who cares where they went for ice cream or what school dance they attended? That I'm on this planet because of a runny nose is all I need to know.

I'm not a fan of the "love at first sight" story. It's too short, there's no drama. And it's a little arrogant that they just happened to get so lucky. Most people are out there desperately looking for someone to match up with, joining hiking clubs, taking pottery classes, creating inflated online profiles, and still end up alone.

I understand that it really does happen, but those people should really keep it to themselves.

Another reason you should listen to these family stories is that the older you get, the more dirt you hear. There are secret, salacious parts of your family history that they don't tell you until you get older. I had a great-aunt and -uncle who were as cute as an old couple could be. The story of how they met and fell in love was the stuff of storybooks.

What I found out later was how Uncle Lou also fell in love with a stripper in town and left his family for a good three years so he could live in her flat, making love, drinking wine, and pretending that he didn't have a family. Now, to me, that's a much more interesting story, but it doesn't go with the loving narrative and is definitely not something you want to tell the kids at Thanksgiving.

Sometimes the storyteller has a senior moment, lets their guard down, and a little extra gossip slips out that you never heard before.

"Your uncles were in the tile business, they laid all of the tile in Newark's Penn Station, until your Uncle Paul shot that guy at the clam restaurant in Bayonne."

The old men in the family always tell a good story because they're making most of it up. Every old guy fought in a war, saved a company from going under, and had dinner with a former president. As they sit there, in their old fishing hats, they aren't relating history as much as telling you that they still matter, that they made a mark on this world. Short spasms of leftover testosterone shoot out and, without even realizing it, they are telling you how they wrestled a great white shark and saved everyone at the aquarium. Even though you know it's ridiculous, all you can do is say, "Wow," and reach for another scoop of crab dip.

The best family stories are the ones they're carrying around about you. They know things about us as small children that even we don't know. How we acted, what we liked, things we did. How we would cry every time we saw that stuffed animal in the corner of our crib. How you would only be happy when your grandmother held you, that she was the only one who could quiet you down. They are the keepers of your first years. So sit back and listen and just let them talk.

We are all nothing more than a collection of stories, so if

they want to tell them again and again, so be it. But always remember: To become the wise old sage of the family, you have to be old. So while they're filling you in on the unknowns of your life with magical tales, keep in mind that there's a good chance they're probably thinking about someone else.

bad family games

Pin the Tail on Grandma
Whac-a-Kid
Trivial Pursuit: Playboy Edition
Pet Hunting
Monopoly
Naked Checkers
Strip Poker
Bong Hits
Drunk Dictionary

birthday parties
belong at home

Families have a lot of reasons to celebrate. There are birth-days, anniversaries, graduations, job promotions, engage-ments, baby showers, and the occasional going-away party for that uncle who's going to live with the Pygmies. And that's a good thing. There should be moments in between the doctor visits, meetings with your boss, and colonoscopies when we squeeze out a little joy with the ones we love.

But if your celebrations are larger than six people and the restaurant can't give you a private room, forget the restaurant, cancel the reservation, and celebrate at home.

At home a family makes sense. They're a herd of people who gather around their usual watering hole, eating the same foods and passing out on their spot on the couch. But out in public that same family becomes a confused stampede out of its element, thrashing around, causing nothing but trouble. There's nothing scarier than seeing a large family stomping into a restaurant with stacks of presents and Mylar balloons. This is not the making of a good time. This is the making of a riot.

They burst through the door of the TGI Fridays like pirates

ransacking a town. Parties of two and three scurry out of their way and run for cover. Busboys begin to weep. The hostess stutters as she looks down at the reservation list and checks in the party of twelve she was hoping would cancel.

The first problem is that a group that big takes up a lot of space. Too much space. Anytime they have to start putting tables together and looking for extra chairs, it's a sign that the group would be better off in a public park at a picnic table.

Another sign that they don't belong is the noise. Have you ever sat next to a group that big? You and your date are ready to enjoy some quiet conversation when the party bus rolls in like a screaming bachelorette party wearing inappropriate inflatable hats. They immediately start yelling. They yell about where they are going to sit. They yell their gigantic drink orders. They yell at the waiter. They yell at each other. They yell with their mouths full of all-you-can-eat appetizers. Then they get drunk and yell some more.

Even worse than having to observe this fiasco is having to be a part of it. It's a terrible attempt at a party. No one even wants to be there. The young kids certainly don't. They don't want to be dressed in their uncomfortable formal outfits and have to sit in one place for hours. That's not fun. That only happens in church and school. Now you're going to make them sit at this table and have to listen to the adults talk about politics and real estate?

And what kind of party sticks all of their guests at a long table? If you were having a party at home, would you invite people over and then force them to sit in one chair, for three hours, where they can only talk to the people next to them? No. Unless you are into some weird S-M interrogation thing, you wouldn't.

So now you're stuck with the people you're sitting next to and, chances are, they won't be the good ones. Let's face it, in any group of more than six people there're going to be some who are kind of lame and some who are even worse. And there you are, trapped between these jellyfish who have nothing to say. You can do your best to survive, but trying to keep a conversation going with them is like throwing stones into a pile of wet mud.

And, to make matters worse, you hear laughter coming from the other end of the table. Loud, joyous laughter in response to some great story where all the cool people are, while you sit next to Aunt Sonya and her liver breath.

Then the ordering. Holy crab cakes, the ordering! I can't handle it. It takes too long! Way too long! If everyone knew what they were doing it would be a mess, and now add in all these people who act like talking to a waiter is like communicating with an alien being.

The children who don't know how to order from a menu have been left on their own, at the kid end of the table, and now they have to do the two things they fear the most: talk to a stranger and make decisions on the fly. The waitress looks at them and first they freeze, then they panic, and finally, in a moment of desperation, they order the lobster tails and knock over all the water glasses.

The old people are even worse. This is the one place where someone still has to listen to them, and they go all-out. It doesn't matter that they're confused and can't see or hear. It doesn't matter that they have a list of dietary restrictions a mile long. They are there to be served like the kings and queens they were in the old days and this waiter is going to have to listen to them. Not just their waiter. Every waiter working every station and every busboy, cook, valet, even the guy at the next table is, in their old mind, there to serve them. I cringe every time they start waving their wrinkly hand and blurting out orders.

"I want a cocktail. Does the bartender know how to make a Rusty Nail? The right way?"

"I don't know, I can check," mumbles the sixteen-year-old waiter.

"What about a highball? I had a highball when I was in Chicago once. It was cold and rainy. I was at the zoo. Or was it the opera? What were we talking about?"

Shut up and order it, you imbecile! You're not alone. You're in a group. Get it together and move it along. Why doesn't someone take control and tell this group of babbling idiots that everyone is getting water and be done with it? I'll tell you why: because no one is in charge! If we had a leader with any brains we'd be at home right now.

This party is already a mess and the food hasn't even come out yet.

When it does, what are the chances that this poor waiter is going to get everything right? What are the odds that someone at this table won't be screwed out of their chicken fingers? What are the odds it's going to be me? Very high!

But for the good of the team I will not send it back. I'm not slowing things down. I don't send anything back. That's just more time. I have eaten an entire dish of wet fish with a side of cold beets that I didn't order and I never said a word. I'll choke down whatever I have to as long as it gets us closer to the cake.

The cake is a sign that we're getting close to leaving. Bring it out, put candles on it, and start singing. Have you ever noticed that "Happy Birthday" is the longest song ever written? Forget "The Star-Spangled Banner," forget "Stairway to Heaven"; singing "Happy Birthday" in a crowded restaurant literally slows time.

Everyone in the entire restaurant rolls their eyes, one person claps, and we all dig in to the dessert that eighty-year-old Grandpa just spit all over, trying to blow out the candles.

All that's left to do is get the check and fight over who's paying. In a panic, everyone takes out their reading glasses and starts doing long math on their cellphones, screaming about who ate what and how many drinks they've all had. I always keep extra cash on me, because whatever tip this group comes up with for this struggling waiter is not going to be nearly enough.

This wasn't a celebration, it was something to be endured. But finally we are free to go, until someone suggests the worst thing anyone could suggest at this moment.

"Why don't we open the presents here?"

That's when I call the waiter over and order a bottle of tequila and a gun.

fun family traditions

Christmas Caroling
Baking Cookies
Waffle Week
Thanksgiving Parade
Family Reunion
Naked Fudge Races
German Clog Humping
Chihuahua Races
Pole-Dancing Tuesdays
Hide the Grandma

husbands

What is a husband? A whole man, who is one-half of a marriage. The loud, hairy half. He saw someone, fell in love, and decided to live with them for the rest of his life. Where they are headed he does not know but one thing is clear as he looks in the bathroom mirror, sucking in his gut: "I am a husband now."

Becoming a husband is a choice. You are born a son, a brother, a second cousin once removed, but you decide to become a husband. Like many choices that the average man makes, he doesn't put a lot of thought into it, rather he just jumps in and hopes that it will all work out.

He can't sit down and evaluate all the pros and cons because when he's single it's impossible to comprehend all that's involved. There are no classes you can take, they don't hand out pamphlets in the jewelry store when you're buying the ring. All he really knows for sure is that he really likes her body.

It's a confusing time to be a husband, especially in America, because a husband's role is in flux. This is new. This is recent. This has only been happening within my lifetime.

Previously, the husband was the head of the household. It was his job to provide for his family and protect his wife and children. In return, he was the king of the castle.

That has changed.

There are no roles anymore, it's all improv. The positive effect of progress is that after years of following the orders of idiots, wives are no longer expected to obey their husbands and a husband isn't expected to make more money than his wife. It's all hands on deck as everyone tries to do anything to survive. These are positive changes but have left many men confused about how they are supposed to act.

There is some perplexing information out there for guys, in magazines and on websites, filled with lists of what men should and should not do. "The Top Ten Things a Man Should Do for His Wife Without Asking," "The Top Fifty Things a Husband Should Stop Doing Immediately," "Why Are Men So Stupid?", "Who Needs Men Anymore?"

The problem is that all these articles are written by women. This is a helpful expression of what women want but is not a realistic take on what men can do. What men are hearing is that a wife wants her husband to act like a man—not necessarily the man he is, but the man that she wants him to be.

Good luck.

A lot of this leads to husbands trying to fake it. If a wife wants him to be more sensitive, that's fine, but he's going to have to pretend. You're talking about a different kind of animal. I would like my cat to chase Frisbees, but it's not going to happen.

Wives ask for men to be more involved with the children, which isn't a lot to ask. What is a lot to ask is that he care about the children as much as she does. No man can decide to be more maternal; it's just not possible.

I love my children, but it doesn't compare to what my wife feels. When we go out for the night, as soon as she gets in the car, she gets all misty-eyed.

"I miss them already," she says.

I don't even know who she's talking about.

Here is the trickiest part of being a husband. All of the really great aspects that a husband gets out of a marriage are so emotional he can't talk about it. He can't. He feels it, he knows it, but to start talking about it is nearly impossible.

Guys don't hang out with other guys and talk about how much they love their wives. If they did, the other guys would down their beers and head for the exits. We just don't do it. We don't cuddle up with our buddies under a blanket and spend time talking about how lucky we are and how warm we feel inside. It's hard to even type that.

Because we don't talk about our marriage and unearth it and evaluate it, a lot of times wives feel unloved. They feel like we aren't paying enough attention or spending enough time working on "us."

But a husband is working on it all the time; he's just not talking about it. The one thing husbands have going for them in a marriage is that they are goal-oriented and that's a real positive, because whatever we do, we want to be good at it. Therefore, we want to be the best husband we can possibly be.

Whatever that means.

there are no great guys

There are no great guys. This is an important fact that every woman needs to know. Chances are, at some point in your life, you will have to deal with a man. If you are ever going to consider dating a man, marrying a man, or coming within twenty feet of a man, this is really important stuff.

I tell my daughters this fact every day, and I truly believe it. There are no great guys. Good guys, sure. There are good guys, really good guys who are trying to be great. But there are no great guys.

American men are probably as good as you're going to get. We're trying. We really are. We're wearing diaper bags and fighting for equality and telling you we want equal pay, but you have to keep in mind that it's an act. It is a role we are trying to play because we know it will make you happy. We are trying to become a soft, cuddly, understanding version of ourselves, but you must realize that inside all of us is a barbarian who wants to burn the village to the ground.

Men are ruthless and aggressive and powerful. That's how we kept wild animals from eating the children, and built dams and roads and villages. It's how steel got made and bent into skyscrapers. How tunnels were dug underneath rivers and through the sides of mountains.

We are beasts who, since the beginning, did whatever we had to do to get the planet and the universe to submit to our will. It may have given us global warming, strip malls, and turned the earth into concrete, but it also made the place pretty livable.

This is in us. It is in our blood. It is how we are made. This is why putting this animal instinct aside and acting like a "great guy" is a fraud.

My wife was happy that her friend was getting married to a "great guy."

"He's a great guy, she's so lucky he's really, really great."

No, he's not. I haven't even met him and I know he's not. He might be great at hiding his evil ways, but he's not great.

So keep that in mind. If you have a man, if you are married to a man, you are with a wild animal. A man is a wild animal. He may look like a gentleman, but he is just a gorilla who knows how to dress.

So use him wisely. Don't be stupid with your man. Don't ask us to do certain things. Don't ask us to watch the children. Would you ask a bear to watch your children? You should know that we don't *really* watch the children. Not the way that you watch the children. We watch them eat bottle caps and fall down stairs, and we laugh and high-five our friends.

Don't ask me to shop for clothes with my thirteen-year-old daughter. I shouldn't be in Forever 21 waiting for my daughter to come out of the dressing room. No one in the store knows that I have a daughter in the dressing room! They just see a sweaty, uncomfortable man breathing heavily by himself next to the underwear section.

And I shouldn't pick the young one up from gymnastics. I shouldn't be with all the moms waiting for class to be over. They're all chatting away about playdates and schedules, and all I'm doing is wondering which one of these moms would I have sex with first. I apologize, but that's where our head goes. And this isn't a matter of *which* mom, because I would have sex with *all* of them—the weird one, the one with the thing on her eye—but which one first, while I have the energy.

I know, we're not the best.

In the cartoons of yesteryear, men were often depicted as wolves. A wolf in a suit and tie, with his giant tongue hanging out, drooling on the sidewalk, and the minute a woman walked by, his eyes would pop out of his head, and he'd start stomping his feet, panting, and punching himself in the face. It is a ridiculous, insulting assumption that this is how all men act deep inside, but one that could not be more accurate if God had sketched it out herself. We are wolves. Drooling, cunning wolves.

We have to spend an entire lifetime trying to get that hellhound to behave and act less wolflike. Any place where a man has to behave with manners and civility, such as business trips, dance recitals, and parent-teacher conferences, is a struggle. It takes practice. It is not something that comes naturally to us.

What does come naturally is trying to write our name in the snow by peeing on it and scratching ourselves in and around our testicles. We also like spitting through the air to see how far it can go, and if it can go as far as what we just shot out of our nose.

You should also know that men lie, not always about big things with major consequences, although men do that, but consistently about little things. I'd say it's just for fun but it's not even fun. That's not why we do it, we just do it. To say that I understand it or have a good reason for it would be lying and yet as I write this, I think that might be a lie too.

This is really important for young women to know, especially my daughters. Because they will be interacting with the worst type of guys: young ones. These are the raw, unwieldy makings of a man. They are the awful ingredients that have to be tamed and controlled and beat into submission. They are the wild dogs that have yet to be domesticated. When it comes to girls, and trying to be with a girl, and trying to get a girl to like them back, they will stop at nothing.

Before a young man is taught to be a respectful gentleman, who puts the needs of others before himself, and is sensitive to the needs of others, he is a mere vessel for some pretty potent DNA that is struggling for survival. The DNA wants to procreate in order to survive. DNA will do whatever it has to, to get you to sleep with him. DNA will text you lies, pretend to be someone else, and tell you, "It's okay, we'll just cuddle." DNA is a con man in a cheap suit, who makes for a horrible date.

A young guy is like a dog that sees an unattended steak, just sitting on the floor. I don't care if this is a well-trained show dog with a master's degree from obedience school, the minute he sees that meat, ancient instincts from his wolf past kick in and before his owner can get the *n* out in *no*, the dog will be pooping it out in the yard.

You think you know your man, but you don't. I see them when they're free. When they aren't being watched. When they have nothing to lose and no one to correct them. It's not pretty. It's crude and disgusting behavior and apparently it can get you elected president.

Now, don't get me wrong. Men are fun. Men are a blast. Men come up with fun ideas like tying an inner tube to the back of a boat and dragging your friend across the lake. Men came up with the polar bear challenge, chugging beer through a funnel, and hot-dog-eating contests. I don't have the scientific evidence or research to back this up, but I will go out on a limb and declare with total confidence that it was a man who first lit his farts on fire.

Men will also look out for you, and protect you. When my wife was pregnant and we walked through the streets of New York, I was shoving people out of the way. Men, women, policeman, I didn't care and I didn't think. I just acted on instinct. If you came within twenty feet of my wife, I was going to knock you out.

When the baby was born it only got worse. My wife would put the baby in the stroller and I would literally walk ahead of them, leading them through the crowded streets, like a bodyguard fending off the paparazzi.

We are hardwired to protect those around us, and not with intellect, but with strength and fists and biting. Think about your man for a minute. Where does he keep his weapon? Yes. His weapon. Oh, he has one. I don't care if he's the type who spends a lot of his time listening to NPR and baking brownies in a cozy sweater, preaching against the NRA, I guarantee you he has a bat or a golf club, and he knows where it is, and has fantasies about how he would, or rather, how he *will* use it when the bad guys show up.

I'm not going to tell you what weapons I have because if you come over I don't want you to have any advantage. But, trust me, there are many, and they are strategically placed around the house, just waiting for you to show up uninvited.

We all have fantasies about how it all goes down when the stuff hits the fan and I see myself clearly grabbing my weapon, doing an impressive spin move, and taking you out before you even know I'm in the room. I'm not sure why I have to spin, but you might as well look good when you're kicking some major ass.

This built-in bodyguard that you get when you are with a man is great, but it doesn't make him a great guy. It's really just part of his job. The fact that we all have weapons and really, really want to use them definitely drops us from the "great" category back down to "kind of good."

Look, the reality is, we are all flawed. Nobody is perfect, and, really, the guys are just a little worse than the women (but a whole lot more destructive). If I can let my daughters know that the person they will one day fall in love with isn't that great, then I will have done my job. And it will be better for everyone because I won't have to break out my hidden lead pipe and Japanese throwing stars to defend them.

don't drag him to an art gallery while on vacation

Don't make him do it. You know he doesn't want to, so why torture him? To prove that he loves you? Hasn't he done that already? He married you, had children with you, remembered your anniversary, and even took you away for a romantic get-away. And this is how you repay him? By making him get up off the lounge chair, leave the hotel pool, and go to a local art gallery while he's on vacation? Leave the man alone.

Look, if you want to go to a tourist art gallery, go. Why bring this big lug with you? So he can sulk around making those sighing noises he makes when he wants to leave but is too scared to say so? Do you really need the pressure to leave when he is standing outside on the curb? You know how he can get, so why invite that energy into the gallery with you to just look at paintings of lighthouses and stupid ocean birds?

Let me be clear, it's not every art gallery. If the two of you are in New York or even Omaha, for that matter, and you want to go to a museum, then we have something to talk about. He should have to go to that and have some culture rammed down his buffalo wing–eating throat. But he should be allowed to skip these overpriced tourist traps filled with painted sunsets, scattered shells, and, if they're getting really deep, maybe some footprints in the sand.

They're just using elements of your trip to sucker you into a sale because they know when we are on vacation we get carried away and do things that we shouldn't. That's why white girls come home with cornrows, dads with Hawaiian shirts, and moms with bad, overpriced artwork. It's not being with you that he is trying to avoid, it's being ripped off when you're all boozy on piña coladas and fish tacos.

Maybe if I explain the story of these seaside "artists," you'll understand. He doesn't love to paint; he loves to get tourists to hand over their credit cards.

He probably started out with a pretty decent ability to paint, not amazing but at least better than his brothers' and sisters', and that went to his head. When school got a little more difficult and he couldn't keep up in math, he didn't work harder and try to improve his grades, he did the opposite. He let them slip because he knew that he was an artist, man. That's what he said in between bong hits.

He was going to live in SoHo and take a lover and live on the edge. He was going to live in paint-splattered overalls and old work boots that curve up at the ends from all those hours squatting over the giant canvas. The canvas that he would make love on and then tear to shreds with an X-ACTO knife because artists always had X-ACTO knives because X-ACTO knives are cool.

But when he went to the big city it didn't work out. He would have had to compete with the thousands of other artists who also painted better than their siblings. This would take work. He doesn't like work. He was good at the drinking and getting high part, but as far as the art stuff, he just couldn't keep up.

He took the bus back home to New Jersey and didn't pick up a brush for months.

"What's the point?" That's what his father yelled to him as he saw his son getting high on a beanbag chair, watching daytime television. "A struggling artist isn't an artist if he just sits around all day. That's just a bum."

That's when he decided, out of spite, to prove his father right and go where bums go: the beach. There he got a stupid job and a stupid apartment and hung out with stupid people and drank in a stupid bar.

Until one night, when he was doodling on a cocktail napkin and a vacationing divorcée cozied up next to him and complimented his doodle.

"Oh, this? This is nothing," he said.

"No, you're really good," she said as she touched his arm.

And that night he might not have made love like Jackson Pollock on a giant splattered canvas, but he did some heavy petting at the bar with a total stranger, as his cocktail napkin stuck to her back, and that was enough to get him painting again.

He started with a sunset. Then he added some rocks with a little light bouncing off the sand. He bought some postcards at the T-shirt shop and started copying those scenes as well. He displayed them at the farmers market and the tourists bought them all. "These people will buy anything!" he said to the bartender as he ordered another beer. "What a bunch of morons!"

And now he sits every day, with his *Breaching Whale* and

Crabs Dancing on a Rock, waiting for the next tourist that he can fool.

Now, you might see this con man as innocent and entering his gallery as just something to do. That's okay, but just do it by yourself. Your husband can't be in there without wanting to punch this guy in the nose.

Leave your husband at the pool where he can nap and dream of all the fun things the two of you will do together when you get back. If he's still asleep when you return, head down to the beach and have your hair put into cornrows.

things husbands lie about

How much money they have
How much money they spent
How much money they make
How much money the tickets cost
How much money they donated
How much money they tipped
How much money their bonus was
How much money golf cost
How much money they spent at Hooters
How tall they are

you aren't marrying
who you think you are

If you think that you are thinking about all the right things when you're thinking about whether or not you could marry the person who you've been sleeping with, think again.

Forget how attracted you are to them, and how nice and funny they are. You need to think long and hard about the future. The distant future.

This guy with the motorcycle and the strong arms is not the person who you will end up with. This girl with the super-cool attitude, who loves football as much as you, will not be with you for long.

Whoever you're with will eventually be replaced by a vastly different version of this person. You must do your best to picture who that will be. Look at their parents and try to visualize who they will become after nature and time gets done with them.

Look at your man.

Now picture him with no hair. Just do it. No hair or, worse, just several strands, like a doll that's been caught in a fire. Now make him fat. He doesn't have to be enormous, but picture him with a three-inch layer of marshmallow covering his entire body.

Now put him in sandals. Yes, sandals. Maybe they're the type that he thinks are cool with Velcro straps, but they're still sandals and he's going to wear them. Sometimes he'll wear them with socks, because it's cold outside in the morning when he's getting the paper and he doesn't want his toes to be cold.

This will be the guiding fashion principle of your man. Easy. Easy elastic waistbands, buttonless shirts, and slip-on shoes.

You know what's not easy? Clipping his toenails. Trimming his nose hair. Making a trip to the eye doctor to get new glasses. That's not easy at all. That takes effort. Effort he doesn't want to make, with energy he does not have. It's much easier to put some tape on them and keep wearing them.

You know what else is easy? Shorts with white tube socks and thick sneakers. That's way easy.

Why should he care about looking good? Where's he going, to the club? Dancing? Out for a night on the town? Nope. He's going to the garage to work on his hobby.

That's right, he has a hobby now. Sometimes he paints birdhouses. Sometimes he glues together plastic models of boats. Sometimes he goes into the garage to install a new miniature cedar tree on the edge of his make-believe town that his train set runs through.

If he's not in the garage he's on his computer looking up Halloween decorations in June, because that's his thing now. Or maybe his thing is the Civil War, and he needs to order another book to put with the fifty other books that he has.

Or maybe he needs to go into a Civil War chat room to talk about a battle while you fall asleep on the couch where you actually thought he might join you for a cuddle.

Are you laughing? Are you thinking, *No way*? Well, I'm laughing that you're laughing because there's a good chance that the future version of your man will be dressed as a soldier at Gettysburg, and he's not laughing at all.

Now look at your woman. That young, beautiful thing. Now take all her hair, whatever style she has right now, and picture it cut shorter and sticking straight up on the top of her head like a doll that was left out in the rain.

She's not into "easy" as much as the man is, but comfortable is definitely a goal. Forget high heels, she wants comfortable shoes that won't hurt her corns. She also needs some big, comfortable bras and underpants. No more lace bras and panties; now she wears giant cotton get-the-job-done underpants that she hand-washes in the sink and lets dry on the shower curtain rod.

The only thing she remembers about fashion is that she likes flowers. So that's what she wears, a big flower on the top of her head, a dress covered in flowers, and a flower on the toe of each shoe, strutting around like a piece of movable wallpaper.

She'll still do her makeup the way she always does, but the effect isn't quite the same because her lips and eyes are in a slightly different place. Now she looks slightly more like a circus clown trying to catch the bus during a hailstorm.

Her hobby is shopping. She may not like shopping now, but the future version of her will learn to love it because there's so much to do there. She can look at stuff, have a tea, see some friends, and get in her steps. All while being away from you.

I'm not saying that there is anything wrong with the future version of your partner, I actually find it charming and reassuringly content. I'm just pointing out that this is who you will end up with and they're coming much quicker than you think and will be around much longer than this young version who you've fallen in love with.

I know that my wife is going to be about five inches shorter, wearing giant eyeglasses, and covered in animal hair, but I like what I see.

So, if you see this version of your lover in your mind and you're okay with it, then by all means, go ahead and marry them. And until death do you part.

john is dead

Welcome to the Sunny Vale Funeral Home, for the funeral of John Green. It is my duty, as the funeral director, to give his eulogy, because no one who knew him bothered to come. He was a father, a husband, a son, a brother, a dog owner, and according to his sister, "He hated every minute of it."

By all descriptions John was a bad man whom no one liked and apparently that was just fine with him.

He lived in Park Ridge, New Jersey, his entire adult life, and was known in the neighborhood as the man who lived in the house, at the end of the street, who threw apples at pets, hurled profanities at children and lit Mrs. Scott's mailbox on fire. His was the one house you didn't go to on Halloween or you'd end up sprayed with a hose and hit with acorns.

If any of his three children were willing to make the twenty-minute drive here today, I'm sure they would shed a tear or two. His eldest son remembers John as that man who smoked in the dark and ate by himself. His daughter, Carol, felt suffocated by his presence and she left home "as fast as I could." And Billy, the youngest, was surprised to hear from us, having thought that John had died back in the Clinton years.

He held his own unique beliefs. He didn't think that a man his age should have to recycle, choosing instead to let the garbage man sort it out. He didn't believe in global warming, because his feet were always so damn cold all the time. And he never tipped anyone, saying that he would only consider it when everyone started doing their goddamn job.

The only thing John did like, apparently, was practical jokes that only he found funny. He put fake parking tickets on cars, pretended to have heart attacks to scare his wife, and hid shrimp in his son's closet, which was a joke that continues to smell to this day.

He leaves behind his wife, Linda, who apologizes that she couldn't be here today, but she is currently celebrating on a Royal Caribbean cruise to the Galápagos Islands. She did, however, send this message.

"I was married to John for forty-five years. That's a long time, but trust me, it felt even longer. They say a marriage is a funny thing, but ours was not. When I met John he was a young man filled with promise and hope and a full head of hair. What he turned into was a bald, spiteful blob, filled with jealousy and anger.

"On his deathbed he called himself a family man, but I'm not sure whose family he was talking about. He only cared about himself and would have been better off living alone doing the only thing he enjoyed: painting those godforsaken birdhouses of his.

"I know it's not nice to say that you're happy when someone dies, so I'll just say that I'm extremely pleased that I'll never have to eat breakfast with him again."

So that was John. He was surrounded by friends and family but was completely alone. Which makes today a somewhat joyful occasion, as lying in this coffin by himself seems to be his wish come true.

At this point I would normally give directions to the cemetery, but you guys work here, so, Bob, why don't you drive and we'll wrap this thing up.

wives

You can't be a wife if you're not a woman and that is why a wife is such a powerful, mysterious, and wonderful thing. They are resilient, sensitive, and profoundly complex.

They are soft, thoughtful, and kind. They are the giving, nurturing mothers of us all. But make no mistake: They are killers.

A wife does not suffer fools. She will get rid of a lifelong friend just from an eye roll at dinner.

"Did you see how that witch looked at me?"

And you'll never see her again. She'll be out of the picture frames, deleted from the contacts, gone, like old-time Russia. Do you know how scary that is for a man? To know that everyone in your life is on a giant roulette wheel of death, and that we're on there too, riding along at double zero?

That's terrifying to a man because men never get rid of their friends. Ever. A guy's friend could be the biggest jackass in the world. He could become an alcoholic, a drug addict, rob a liquor store, go to jail, come out ten years later, come to *his house, pee in his pool, hit on his wife and they'll pick up like old friends.*

"That's Don! Look what he's doing to the mailbox. He's hilarious."

A wife would never put up with that. She has a focus that her husband will never have.

But I'm suspicious of men who say they don't understand their wives. It's a cop-out to say that women are unknowable and therefore not worth paying attention to. I would argue that it's not that they don't understand women, but that they forgot.

When I was a child, the women in my life were infinitely more interesting and thoughtful than the men. At family gatherings my father and the other husbands would sit in silence for hours in front of the TV. When they did talk it was serious and blunt, not so much a conversation as a bunch of guys telling each other how it is. It always had something to do with the size of their engines or what that jerk of a president did or what idiotic play the stupid coach just called. This was followed by more silence, while they scratched and thought about money and who they're going to knock out next.

But when I would wander into the kitchen, where the wives were all gathered, it was like a party. The conversations were funny, cutting, and alive. They talked about things with levels and depth. They were animated; they cried and they laughed and they were not afraid of their emotions because, unlike men, being emotional wasn't a sign of weakness, it was just what they did.

I loved being in that room because I could be funny there. I would tell stories, make jokes, and do impressions. If

I tried to do that in the room with the Jets game on, I'd get punched. Not only were they an amazing audience, but many of them were even funnier than I was.

But, as I got older, something changed and I started spending more time watching the game with the men. I remember the day that my Aunt Gloria noticed that I wasn't participating in their conversations. I came in to get a glass of water and they asked me to do one of those funny voices that made them laugh so much, and I refused.

"Oh, no. Look at him," she said. "Tommy doesn't want to talk with us anymore. Oh, no, he's a man. Look at him, he's going back with the men."

Her definition of a "man" meant that I had become just like the rest of the men in her life. The guys in the other room who were thickskulled, sitting in front of another endless game, didn't tell jokes, and only pretended to listen or, even worse, just rolled over and went to sleep.

For a while I was a promising example that not all men just grunt about gas mileage or how to beat the traffic. For a while I was a guy who liked to talk to them, who found them silly, but not as their husbands did, not as a nagging wife, but silly in all the best ways.

But as I grew into a man and had to compete with other men, I guess I grew more stoic, more masculine and detached. I could feel that sitting around with the women made me seem weaker and more feminine in the eyes of other men. Men firm up, stand strong, play it close to the vest, close off, and shut down. But the reality is, it's the people who retreat who are the most frightened. Most of the time, silly is stronger.

I never developed a need to talk about the type of engine

in my car, I don't even know what it is, but I do find my-self, at times, reacting to my wife the same way other hus-bands do: with a slight touch of annoyance and a dismissive shrug. Men sometimes seem oblivious to their wives, but that's because we're too busy staring at our own belly buttons and wondering about the stock market to pay attention.

Imagine how much stronger and in tune men would be if they continued to be truly more open to the women in their lives, particularly their wives. I'm not saying it's easy dur-ing the everyday scrum to drop what we're doing, but we could open our eyes a little wider.

I saw Jane Goodall speak in Vancouver, at the Univer-sity of British Columbia. Here was this tiny, eighty-three-year-old woman who was so powerful and impactful without ever raising her voice. She didn't have to. Her actions, her resolve, and her morality all came through and shone on the world in a display of power that only a woman could show.

As she talked about her organization, and how they are trying to save endangered species, it suddenly occurred to me who is endangering them. It's men. Angry, thoughtless, men-acing men, circling on motorcycles, shooting their guns in the air, trying to make a buck and threatening to tear every-thing down in their path.

And yet she prevails.

As a wife.

As a mother.

As a woman.

the wife lie detector

Your wife knows when you are lying. You should consider this a good thing. Without her, how would you ever know when you're wrong? Seriously, isn't it a relief to know that when you are telling a story you have someone there who stands ready to correct your every detail?

When I was on my own I had no way of knowing how wrong I was about everything. My friends never corrected me. They just let me blab on and on. They must not have cared about me as much as my wife. Think about it. All the people you work with probably just chuckle when you tell a story. How uncaring.

But your wife cares. She stands ready, like an investigator waiting to pounce on any inconsistency in a suspect's story. I could tell a story about how my flight almost went down, forcing us to crash-land outside of Reno, where I had to jump on that slide to the tarmac, partially covered in fire, and how I was forced to spend *twelve hours* in the hospital next to the pilot who lost both his eyes. At the end of that tale, my wife would get everyone's attention and let them know that I actually spent *eleven* hours in the hospital.

144 | your dad stole my rake

Does this detail matter to the story? No. Is it an interesting tidbit of information? Not at all. But you see, my wife is a perfectionist. When I tell a story in front of her I feel like I'm testifying before a Congressional Subcommittee on Factual Storytelling.

"Do you, Mr. Papa, solemnly swear to tell the truth, the whole truth, and nothing but the truth?"

"No. No, I don't. I'm just trying to get through this dinner party with these people. No one has told a good story yet and I figure if I could just get a couple laughs, that should ride us through dessert and we can get out of here."

A story needs flow. It needs rhythm. It doesn't need to be stopped dead in its tracks to correct that something cost ten dollars instead of eight!

The real reason a wife does this is that she's a little angry with your embellishments. And why shouldn't she be? All your cute little attempts at being charming and your blatant bending of the truth is how she got into this mess in the first place. My wife realizes now that I'm not as great as I made myself out to be. When we were dating I put on a show and she fell for it but now she realizes she was fooled.

What was I supposed to do? Show her the real me? The guy who doesn't have the working man's ability to fix anything and at the same time lacks the nerdy income-generating abilities of Bill Gates? No way. The one thing I could do was tell a good story, and I told her a doozy and now she's mad and sees it as her duty to not let other people be scammed as well.

It's as if she just discovered that the Scarecrow in *The Wizard of Oz* is really just a guy in a hay suit and she's going to tell everyone about it.

Look, on some subjects, like raising the children, I am

more than happy to accept her corrections. This is her domain, and while there are stories about certain events that took place over certain years where it feels like we might have raised different children in different countries at different times, she is the keeper of the truth. I'm not talking about trivial events here, either. I'm talking about our babies' first steps, their first words, and whom we named the children after. There are entire stories about family vacations that I have no memory of.

She can have those. She has the memory of an elephant and I, a brain you would find in a goldfish. Even though I can see my memories as clear as day, I have to believe that she's right. It also means a lot more to her that she is right, so rather than challenge her I just shut my trap.

There are some important stories that I do push back on. The legendary story of our first kiss is up for dispute. I can tell you with all confidence that we were on Second Avenue outside of H&H Bagels where I hailed her a cab and before she got in she turned and attacked me. I'm not complaining at all, but to hear her tell this story, I made the first move before our bagels hit the plate.

I am sticking with my version of this story because I know it's true and it's the one story that I feel I should be allowed to own. She can interrupt my stories with minor corrections and kill a good joke in the name of accuracy, but when I tell the fable of our first kiss, I will hold my ground, because she was totally all over me.

And it makes for a better story.

the importance of the forced romantic getaway

Romance is the key element in the beginning of every relationship. It's what drives the whole union. You meet, there is a chemical reaction, and, like two electric eels, you twist and dance and turn each other on. (I think that's what eels do. If they don't, I'm not sure why they're here.)

But then this romance leads to marriage and children, and buying a house, and adopting some pets, and you begin making car payments, paying for school, carpooling, and spending weekends at gymnastic meets, and traveling to baseball games, and suddenly there is very little time for romance.

You ultimately become business partners in a horrible non-profit organization. You're doing good work. There's a lot of love there and you're helping people, but in order to achieve that romantic feeling that at one time came naturally, you now need a plan.

Welcome to the Romantic Getaway.

They're goofy, and forced, and far from spontaneous, but if you want a healthy marriage you have to do it. Call your parents, beg a friend, hire a sitter, and have them come to watch the kids. All you have to do is get over the embarrassment of waving goodbye while you're all aware that you're heading off to a hotel to have sex.

Actually, you don't have to be that embarrassed because here's a little secret about the Romantic Getaway: At a certain point it's not as much about the sex as it is about the sleep. You enter the peaceful serenity of an empty hotel room, without children and responsibility, and your brain literally disconnects. Before you even know what's happened, it's the next day and housekeeping is knocking on the door, telling you it's checkout time.

A bed-and-breakfast is a favorite place for the Romantic Getaway, but I've always found that to be extremely creepy. If sex is what you're after, a house built in the 1700s with a bed as creaky as a rusty wagon isn't the most carefree and uninhibited environment. That's always a creepy morning, coming down and sharing coffee with all the strangers who were eavesdropping on you the night before.

"Well, good morning, cowboy. Hi-ho, hi-ho," says your irritated neighbor.

It's like getting caught at your parents' house.

Recently, my wife has been insisting that we go to spa resorts. These places are a work of genius. Let's build a hotel with a golf course *and* a giant spa. He gets to golf and she gets the massage that he doesn't want to give her. It's foreplay by surrogate. Everybody wins!

The one kink in this perfect system is if you don't golf. I play a little but not enough to leave my wife, in the middle of a vacation, for five hours without a guilt-free conscience. She sees this as an opportunity to drag me to the spa with her.

"Come on, we'll get a couple's massage, it will be great. Just relax and let your mind wander, it's wonderful."

It is not wonderful. Maybe for my wife, but I'm a man. A naked man. Being touched by a strange new lady. If I let my mind wander the way it wants to, it's going to show. So the whole time I'm in there, I'm thinking about death and taxes and slow dancing with my grandfather. By the time I'm done I'm more tense than when I went in.

"Yeah, that was great. I'll be back at one o'clock for the sandpaper loofah on my nipples."

The thing about these romantic getaways is that, despite all the awkwardness, they really do work. We are so much happier when we return home to the battlefield and it really doesn't matter where you go. Just go—anywhere, a hotel in the next city, a Motel 6 off the freeway, even that creepy motel in town that looks like a serial-killer boot camp.

We once stayed in our minivan while it was parked in the garage at our own house. We couldn't find anyplace to go, so we pulled in, shut the garage door, waited to see if the kids could hear us, and had our own secret getaway, ten feet from our kitchen. We were out of the house, we were together; it counts.

It's all about spending time alone. Not on the couch. Not brushing your teeth. Not those couple of minutes while the kids do the dishes. You need time to get past the logistical conversations of running a household and reach back to who you were as a new couple.

That couple who laughed together and really wanted to hear each other talk, because the talk was about the two of you, not pet vaccinations and clogged toilets. Back when you asked each other questions that had nothing to do with whether you locked the doors, or picked up the kids, or saw that rash on the dog's ass.

It's a real balancing act that the only person you are legally allowed to be romantic with is the same person who may be yelling at you about how you load the dishwasher. That's why it's imperative that you leave those roles behind, and as soon as you pull out of the driveway.

What doesn't count as a romantic getaway is any trip that involves any of your family. You can't call anything a "getaway" if it involves bringing the people you're trying to get away from.

Your family is needy and judgmental and should be left at home. When you are holed up alone in a hotel together the only person who can judge you is the waiter delivering your room service. When you open the door in a robe, for the fourth order of chocolate-covered strawberries and the fifth bottle of champagne, sure, he's going to judge you, but, unlike your mother, he's not allowed to say anything about it.

So just go. Every once in a while, when you're starting to get sick of each other, pack a bag, ditch that nonprofit organization, and run away from home.

we'll sleep when
we're dead

There are mistakes in a marriage that can send you flying over the guardrail, flipping down a rocky cliff, and bursting into a ball of flames. You can avoid those major crashes, but everyone hits a speed bump now and then. Those are the smaller mistakes you run into that might make you bottom out but that you can quickly recover from.

One speed-bump mistake is coming into the kitchen in the morning and declaring that you had a great night's sleep. What a stupid thing to say to the person you share a bed with. One person's good sleep comes at the cost of the other's misery, and the idea that you'll both have slept well is as inconceivable as the idea that you will have romantic dinners, followed by hours of lovemaking, on a nightly basis.

"I had a great night's sleep."

"Yeah, *you* did. You snored like a whale with a sinus condition. I was up all night," she says as she slams down your coffee.

Sleeping together is one of the most difficult things you can do as a couple. You are living this difficult life together, filled with backbreaking work. All day long you support each other like dedicated teammates. Exhausted, you crawl into bed, kiss each other good night, then the battle begins.

For every action there is a reaction, and there is no clearer evidence of that than in the bed of a married couple. If she tosses, he turns. If he snores, she listens. If he gets up to wander around in the dark, she waits for his return. The only chance you have of both sleeping soundly is if you go out drinking, come home, and pass out on top of each other.

I heard of a wife who would stop her husband from snoring by punching him in the head while he slept. This actually seems like a pretty good idea. No man really minds getting punched, especially if he's sleeping, and if she could just aim for the arm, why not?

If I roll over on my left side or, as my wife calls it, "the wrong side," and I start snoring, go ahead, haul off and hit me. It's no different from pushing a cow into the barn. You need this beast to move, they're too stupid to figure out what you're saying, so just reach back, grab some fist, and let him have it.

Now, if your wife snores like a jackhammer, I am going to give the radical advice of telling you *not* to punch her. I don't care where we are with gender neutrality; I'm going old-school and saying it's not right to hit a lady, especially one who has access to your bank information. But, hey, a little shove to get her back to her side of the bed isn't so bad.

The size of the bed is important. Very important. When you are young and in love and can't believe this person is actually sleeping with you, any corner of any couch will do. An army cot, a dorm-room floor, even a cardboard box will do just fine, as long as she doesn't ask you to leave.

It's not just a passion thing but a physical thing as well. A twenty-year-old can sleep in a Dumpster full of rocks and all it takes to recover is a simple stretch and a glass of water. If a forty-year-old person ends up sleeping in his car, he'll be so stiff they'll need the Jaws of Life to get him out. So if that same forty-year-old person has to sleep in a full-size bed with his midsize wife, he's going to wake up in a world of pain.

Can we talk for a minute about these beds and their classifications? A "twin" is not a twin, it's a single. They call this miniature mattress a twin because you'll have to buy two and push them together to make something that's only slightly larger than a dollhouse bed. We've all been stuck on a weird vacation when you try to make a bigger bed out of two twins, but all that does is guarantee that one of you will disappear into the crack and not be seen until morning.

A "full-size" mattress is a misleading term as well because it implies that it will accommodate a full-size person, which it will not unless that person is a twelve-year-old with an eating disorder.

The "queen" is accurate because this is a large enough bed for two people to share, but when you share space with your wife she is going to dominate and get what she wants. They could just call this bed a "hers," but why rub it in his face?

The "king" is the big daddy and is named that because it is the only way a husband will have any space to call his own. It's actually just a queen with some extra space that she gives him so he can do whatever weird stuff he does over there.

Whatever size bed you have, it will eventually be turned into a wrestling mat filled with flailing arms and legs, snoring problems, mouth guards, sinus strips, cold feet, hot bodies, and someone getting choked. With all the horrible violence that goes on we're pretty lucky that we're mostly asleep.

I'm not sure why we don't have separate beds, in separate rooms, on different sides of town. It's as if we have to prove that we love each other by sleeping in the same bed, but if the end result is secretly hating each other, then what's the point? It would be much better if we stayed apart for the night, slept well, and had a nice breakfast together. I think deep down this is what most people want and I believe it's also the only reason *I Love Lucy* is still on TV. It's been on the air forever not because it's funny, but because it's exciting to watch this married couple sleeping on opposite sides of the room.

But most of us will never sleep in separate beds. We will be forever entangled in the marriage bed, battling insomnia and fantasies about smothering our spouse with a pillow. So, if you slept well, keep it to yourself, maybe write it down in your journal if you have to, but never say it to your spouse. You're sleeping with the enemy.

that cute thing she does

A good way to analyze whether or not you can go on a second date with a person and then marry them, have children together, and eventually be buried next to each other on a hill somewhere, is to eat with them first.

It's not a mistake that going out to eat with someone is traditionally a first date. You can get coffee, but this isn't going to tell you enough about the real person. Sure, they may be really annoying with a complicated order at Starbucks, but that's everyone at Starbucks. Unless you're like me, a veteran of the road, who orders a black coffee because you're cool like that, and takes pride in grabbing your coffee at the register and walking past all the boobs waiting for their triple-douchey lattes. Sure, the barista may trip you up by making you specify which black coffee, but you'll go with a Pike, which has the added benefit of sounding cool.

Now back to our original programming.

Eating with someone is truly a necessary first test. Let's be clear, these early dates are tests. They are little pass-or-fail activities because we need a lot of information as quickly as possible so we can get on with our lives, with or without this person.

The reason why eating together is so crucial is that if you do continue on, you're going to eat a lot of meals together. That's basically what a relationship is; someone to graze with.

There's breakfast, lunch, dinner, snacks, road-trip gas stations, and vending machines. You will chew gum, slurp soups, twirl pasta, and crunch on Kettle chips together for years to come, and while no one is perfect at any of this, the fewer habits they have that will make you want to kill yourself, the better.

You could meet a beautiful girl with a great sense of humor, who likes the same bands as you, but if she does something weird with her lips when she's sipping from a hot coffee cup, you're in big trouble.

These little trivial eating tics grow in size with every year. That cute little snapping sound your lover makes when they swallow will one day be the loudest sound you've ever heard. Earth-shattering, window-rattling, breaking-the-sound-barrier loud. You have to be okay with that.

We know a couple who have asked us to go on vacation with them. We love these people; they are very good friends of ours, and we will never go. Not because we don't care for them, but because of the way they eat.

They eat with their hands, like monkeys who were raised by baboons on the wrong side of the trees. They hover over whatever is served—spaghetti, chili, soup—and pick it up with their fingers and put it into their mouths. And then they chew, lick, and slurp the ends of their fingers, because they don't use utensils, and put those saliva- and food-covered tentacles back into the food and repeat.

This is bad enough when they are picking at their own plate, but when it is something we are all sharing I have to fight the urge to walk out of the restaurant, jump in an Uber, and drive around the city in search of new friends.

I'm sure they would read this with astonishment and disbelief, as they think it is perfectly normal to run your tongue over your hands like a cat and then shove them back into a communal hummus plate. That's okay that they think this behavior is all right, because they both agree that it's okay and that's why they married each other.

If I had gone on a date with her and she did that, we never would have made it to dessert, but my friend saw this as a sign of compatibility. With each finger lick he jumped for joy inside, thinking, *I've found my soul mate. What are the odds? I use my thumb to spread butter, she uses her thumb to spread butter. It's a miracle!*

Yech.

Look, I'm not perfect. I'm sure there are some habits that I'm unaware of that would make the two of them cringe. But honestly, probably not. I'm pretty flawless when it comes to manners, especially while eating. I follow the long-established rules because I believe those are what keep us humans from regurgitating our breakfast and spitting into each other's mouths like baby birds.

But maybe it's this strict adherence to evolved human behavior that drives my friends crazy. Maybe they think that I'm a tight-ass who's way too obsessed with good behavior.

"Screw Tom and his rules. He's so uptight," they say as they lick salsa off their wrists. "He's no fun at all."

Will we remain friends despite this divide? Yes, of course. Because we are just friends and I can look past the stains on their shirts and the stuff caught in their teeth. But a lover, a partner, or a spouse cannot survive that enormous difference in behavior.

I couldn't turn off the lights at night and lie there in the dark knowing that the person sharing my bed chews with her mouth open. Absolutely not. Is my wife perfect? No, she isn't, but the stuff that she does isn't grounds for divorce because I saw these habits immediately and decided I should call her for a second date.

For instance, I know, when we go into a restaurant together, that we will not be sitting at the first table the hostess gives us. My wife will find something wrong with it, probably having to do with a slight breeze. Her ability to feel a breeze is uncanny. If there is such a thing as the world championships for kite flying she should sign up because she has the ability to detect motions in the air that are so subtle even a mosquito would be impressed.

My wife is funny.

I also know that after we've moved a couple times we will end up back in our original seat having accomplished nothing but having put on a show of musical chairs for the other guests.

Then the waiter will come over and ask, as every waiter has done since the first restaurant was built, if he can get us something to drink. My wife, despite working and eating in restaurants for more than thirty years, will not be prepared for this question. It is a surprise every time. She will stammer and apologize and ask for more time and send him away.

It's cute.

She is a vegetarian, although she eats fish once in a while, but not all fish, especially not the kind of fish that tastes too much like fish. She doesn't remember the names of the fish that she does eat, so when the waiter asks if anyone has questions about the menu she's definitely going to have some. So many, in fact, that he will have to excuse himself from the table in order to catch his breath and start working on his résumé.

He'd better not think it's over when the meal has been completed. If this guy was rattled by the entrée encounter he may be put in the hospital when she orders dessert.

After about twenty minutes of watching my wife try to make up her mind, as if just talking and thinking about the dessert is as enjoyable as actually eating it, she will then move into the most mind-bending part of her order—the tea.

She only drinks tea. Certain teas. Decaf teas. Her favorite is black decaf tea that of course is only carried by two restaurants in all of North America and doesn't exist in every other part of the world. But, God love her, that doesn't stop her from asking. Every time.

Adorable.

He offers alternatives, bringing out the handcrafted wooden tea box filled with a bunch of minty, lemony, no-caffeine herbs and she denies every one. I love watching the look in the waiter's eye when after his entire performance she says no and *then* orders hot water.

"What?" he asks.

"Just a cup of hot water," she replies.

"Just hot water?"

"Yes."

And, before he leaves, she pulls a tea bag out of her purse.

"I brought my own, just in case."

At this point I've seen grown men look at me with tears in their eyes and, unable to speak, mouth the words, "Why? Why?"

Because she's endearing.

Just when you thought the habits were over, we get ready to leave. The bill has been paid and the conversation slows, I will say we should get going, and that's when she will declare that she has to use the ladies' room.

Does this behavior drive you crazy? Are you reading this and thinking that you could never eat or live with a person who acted this way? Well, that's fine. You don't have to. I do, because I love her and she loves me and I saw all of this on the first date and it didn't bother me at all.

what men think their wives do in the bathroom

Shave Their Elbows
Poop Butterflies
Floss Each Tooth Twenty Times
Pluck Their Armpit Hair
Full-Body Moisturizing
Electric Hair Brushing
Roll Around in Flower Petals
Rearrange the Q-Tips
Seaweed Wrap Their Boobs
Make Organic Deodorant out of Fairy Wings

leave the past alone

Husbands and wives should stay off Facebook.

This groundbreaking social media tool that holds all the promise of worldwide connectivity and progress has, like all great technology, become a tool for sex. In this case the first dumb step is looking up every past lover you ever had.

Don't do it. Diving into the past for longer than a fleeting moment is as dumb as keeping that old pair of jeans from high school because you actually think you might fit into them again. Our brain does an amazing job of repainting the past. Everything looks better in our memories. Every apartment was pretty great, every job wasn't so bad, and every girl I was ever with was amazing. They were all witty and funny and beautiful so why not look them up on Facebook and see what they're up to?

Because it's not true! If it was true and they were so great, I would still be with them. The reality is they were annoying, irritating, and didn't like my friends. We broke up for a whole range of reasons, really good reasons, and I don't need to see them ever again. Yet, because of Facebook, I know what they're all doing.

There was one girl who I broke up with because she lived too far away. I lived in New Jersey and she lived in Long Island, New York. If you're going to drive that far and pay all those tolls you'd better really be in love. I wasn't. It was the only time I broke up with someone over the phone. I didn't want to be insensitive, but I couldn't afford to make another trip.

She currently lives in Long Island and is married to a doctor who can easily afford the tolls.

There was another girl who didn't break up with me and I didn't break up with her. It just became obvious that we should move on when she started sleeping with every other guy in the tenth grade. She did it with everybody, every chance she got. She did it under the bleachers at football games, when I was on the field getting my head knocked in. She did it at parties, in the bushes, when I was caught up in a fierce game of beer pong. She did it at her house, right after I left, but just before her mother got home.

She hurt me more than any woman I have ever been with. It took me a long time to figure out why someone could be so cruel when you loved them so much. When I headed off to college I vowed I would never see her again. I haven't, but I did look her up on Facebook.

She currently lives in Long Beach, California, and is married to a guy who, by the looks of things, has no idea what she is capable of.

I think about them all, from time to time, and that's okay. Looking them up on Facebook is not. It's a bad idea. There's nothing wrong with looking in your old photo album and taking a trip down memory lane. At least you can hold it in your hand, sigh, and go back about your life before your wife comes in and finds you.

The problem with Facebook is that it's a living photo album. You click on a picture and a human being appears, and responds, and flirts, and meets for coffee, and suggests you head to a motel on the side of a highway. That's not good at all.

In the old days, time and distance prevented you from making a total fool of yourself. After a breakup, you went about your life and you never saw them again. Maybe, on the off chance, you'd run into each other at an airport. You'd awk-wardly introduce your current spouse, run out of anything to say, and wave goodbye. It was brief and uncomfortable and made you never want that to happen again.

It's not just ex-lovers, either. With Facebook, our history is constantly invading the current day. I would've been much nicer to everyone in my life if I'd known that eventually they were all coming back. It's like we're attending a class reunion every day.

Class reunions were great because you got a chance to see people you hadn't seen in years. You'd see Daryl, the kid who you used to see at lunch, and here he is, a middle-aged guy in an overused suit. You share a drink and think, *Wow, Daryl is hilarious. We should hang out more.*

But by the end of the night, when Daryl is trying to push the soda machine into the Jacuzzi, you realize that maybe giv-ing him your email was a bad idea.

I don't need to watch everybody aging in real time, either. Everyone is getting bigger and fatter, has weird jobs, and live in weird places. They have a GoFundMe campaign going so we can buy them a sailboat in which they can sail around the world. Everyone has old-people problems, money problems, dead relatives, kids in rehab, or they made bad choices and bought a home in a flood zone. Why do I need to hear all this? Just because we had math together thirty years ago?

No, it's better if you get off Facebook altogether. It actually ruins the nice memories you have and is beginning to ruin the present day as well. I know so many people who spend a good portion of their day fighting with everyone they have ever met about politics and health care and global warming. You meet someone at a school bake sale and before you know it they are yelling at you online because you posted something about saving the grizzly bears.

Maintaining a happy relationship with your spouse is a time-consuming, infinitely complex puzzle that takes all the focus and energy that a person can afford. Don't make it more difficult by opening your Facebook page, staring at the empty search field, and entering the name of someone you made out with at the Dairy Queen.

Trust me, they didn't get better with time.

there's no such thing
as a soul mate

We aren't Native American shamans who sit around camp-
fires high on peyote, and you aren't related to the Dalai Lama,
no matter how many hot yoga classes you take. No, we are
just average, run-of-the-mill people whose mystical powers
are no more impressive than that old dream catcher you had
in your window in college. So let's all agree that there's no
such thing as a soul mate.

I like the idea. It sounds very romantic, that your spirit
traveled through another dimension to find this other soul to
go to the movies with, but it runs smack into our grubby,
everyday human existence.

My parents have been together for fifty years, and by most
accounts it's a successful marriage, but calling them soul mates
is a real stretch. If they were a part of something that tran-
scendent, they wouldn't spend every minute reclining on the
couch in their socks, yelling at each other about how loud the
TV is.

There are couples who claim that their relationship is so
much better than everybody else's they just have to be soul
mates. They're not better than everybody else, they're just more

annoying. That these two self-obsessed people hooked up with each other isn't magic, it's just that no one else could stand them.

If it did exist, do you realize how insane the odds would be that you would find your soul mate? Just hooking up with one person who you can deal with out of the seven billion people currently living on the planet is tough enough. Now we are going to include all the people who ever lived and died on the planet? I'm not great at math, but that's got to be in the area of, like, a zillion people.

Let's just walk through what has to be true in order for you to have a soul mate. First, you have to have a soul. You have to have a spirit inside you that either flew through time and space and landed in this body that you are using, or came to be when you were born. This all depends on what religion you're into, what books you've read, or what your older brother came up with while trying to scare you in the dark.

But okay, let's say I have a soul. I'm going to go with the version that I lived here before. I'm a soul from another time. I really like stuff from Europe, so maybe my soul lived in Italy around the Renaissance. Not as a painter or sculptor, but more likely one of the guys who swept the streets or worked in a sausage factory, stuffing the casings. Just a regular knock-around guy who happened to live during the Renaissance but had no idea something special was going on.

So this guy had to die, possibly from some disease like the Black Death or more likely some mishap with a hammer. Something stupid. From there I'd have to go to wherever it is that souls go, like some sort of waiting area, before being summoned back to earth. In my case, I came back in 1970, so

I probably made another quick stop, maybe at the U.S. Civil War, before being kicked to death by a mule.

After all this time traveling, my soul finds its way into this rockin' bod that is writing right now, and magically ends up living in New Jersey, in a one-bedroom apartment, near some train tracks, sleeping next to a German shepherd.

There's more. In order for this soul-mate story to work out, at the same time, my wife's soul had to make its way across the universe and end up in New Jersey too. There, we both go to work in a hotel in the summer, meet in the parking lot, and *whammo*!, soul mate found.

As the kids used to say: "Barf-arama."

This is just BS that's used to sell cheesy posters and lame greeting cards with two longing silhouettes walking at sunset. The kind of malarkey that wedding planners tell their clients— putting some magical spin on their relationship to try to get them to spend more money they don't have.

If you're with someone, you've done enough. You found each other. You overlooked each other's flaws and are working at making it the best relationship, and life, it can be. That's enough. You don't have to inflate it with enchanted spells and *Lord of the Rings* destiny.

My wife and I are two kids from New Jersey, not space travelers separated by centuries. You know what deep, mystical thing I told my friends when I met my wife? "She's hot."

There's nothing you can say about a soul mate that you can't say about a halfway decent couple. "We met and there was instant chemistry." Yeah, chemistry. Two lonely people with recklessly raging hormones, looking to procreate. You don't have to be some witch doctor to figure that out. If you're alone long enough you'll have chemistry with a water bottle.

There's no soul mate. How about you find someone you can tolerate? How about that? Find someone you can sleep next to without throwing up and marry them. You found a brand-new person who likes you enough to take their clothes off and roll around with you. Sure, it's a miracle, but it's not your soul mate.

The only time you should use the term "soul mate" is after you've been with each other for ten years and you have to fill out yet another birthday card, and you just can't come up with something new to say.

Not every relationship has to sound like a fairy tale. You hooked up in a bar, on dollar-shot night, got pregnant, and now live in Chino Hills with two kids and a cat. Congratulations! You did it. You made a life for yourself with a partner who you like enough to make toast for every day.

May your souls live happily ever after.

pets

At some point every family is faced with the decision of whether or not to get a pet. This is one of those horrible ideas that will complicate your life, steal precious minutes from your day, and ruin your house and that you absolutely should do. These animals range in size and shape and amount of hair they leave on your pants, but one thing cannot be denied: They become another member of the family who brings you joy and heartache and, most of the time, is a major pain in the ass.

Some people can't help but get a pet because they love all of God's creatures and the idea of living without an animal is not much of a life at all. My wife is one of these loyal and loving people who enjoys things with tails far more than human beings. Her love for animals truly outweighs her love for people. When she hears the expression "That guy acts like an animal," she thinks it's an insult to the animal.

These types of people think nothing of adopting, breeding, or kidnapping multiple pets. If you're like me and you live with one of those people, then you too will forever be covered in hair.

Many people decide to get a pet for their children. This is a fine idea if you are clear on what "for the children" means. That does not mean "for the children to care for and pay for and raise and train as their own." They won't do any of this and why should you expect them to? They can't even take care of themselves.

If you like animals at all, and hate the idea of them being mistreated, why would you leave them in the hands of an eight-year-old? Anyone who's seen what a child can do to themselves knows that a defenseless kitten doesn't stand a chance in their care.

If you understand that "for the children" means giving them an animal that will lick their faces, love them, and allow them to dress them in hats and sweaters like a human, then, yes, get one for the children.

Not only is it fun but it's a great equalizer for a child. Finally, someone in the house is lower in the pack hierarchy. Not that this always happens. My youngest was very excited to have a dog she could be in charge of, but after a week the puppy grew, started stealing her food, and has been dominating her ever since.

The best reason to bring a beast into your home is for the amount of love that they generate in a family. When my kids show up in the morning on their way to school looking like they are headed to death row and they see our dog, they light up and turn so sweet and lovable that we hardly even recognize them. It's gotten to the point where my wife and I have considered wearing dog collars just to get them to say good morning to us.

Like everything in life, there's a price to pay. Sure, you'll have more love in your home, but you'll also have a lot of hair, vomit, and urine in places that are a great distance from the bathroom. Expensive things that you cherish will be eaten, scratched, and clawed by your pets, often while they are staring you right in the eye. You will never be out of the house for long without thinking that you should race back before they get annoyed and seek revenge on your shoe collection.

Another major change is that you will instantly have a whole new set of chores and places in town where you'll have to go. Places you never even thought about before. Do you spend a lot of time walking around the park with old people? You will now. Do you snicker at the guy who's bent over on the sidewalk picking up feces and carrying it like a purse? Well, who's laughing now?

That pet store that you always drove by and never even saw before is your new hangout. The people who work in that gerbil cage–smelling establishment, filled with plastic toys, crickets, and mice will know you by name because it's about to become your second home.

You also have to pick a vet, because you'll need to visit them and give them big bags of cash on a regular basis. In return for this money they will confuse you, upset you, and send you on your way. I don't put a lot of faith in these vets because they never seem to know what the hell is going on. The most common thing they say is "This is just something they get."

It seems the worse off the animal is, the more useless the vet visits become. I can't tell you how many times we just handed them a credit card so they could run test after test with no results, other than giving us back a dead pet. Then they have the nerve to ask if we want an autopsy for an additional charge. An autopsy on a dead cat that, while it was alive, they couldn't figure out what was wrong with it? It's a little late for that. How about next time we bring in the autopsy guy while the cat is still alive and see if he can tell us what's wrong with her.

I never heard of an autopsy on a cat. Did they suspect foul play? Should we drag the dog in as a suspect and see if he knows anything? He has seemed a little cagey and has been drinking a lot lately; maybe he can't live with the guilt.

I don't mean to sound negative, because I truly do believe that having a pet is worth it, especially in a family. Your house is already a mess, so what are you afraid they're going to ruin? This peaceful oasis filled with kids, in-laws, and Diaper Genies? There's no turning back now. You might as well throw a couple animals into the mix.

"Go ahead, get whatever they want," I said to my wife. And I really don't care. They could get an ostrich and let it loose in the living room. Get some ferrets and see if they fight with the dog. I think it'd be fun.

Frankly, the other day when I was watching our dog eating cat feces out of the litter box, I wished we had gotten an ostrich.

your cat thinks you're too needy

Your cat is totally cool with your relationship. As far as she's concerned, it's really working out just fine. So why are you acting so needy? I know you want more. You're a human being. You need to cuddle and feel loved and appreciated but your cat doesn't. Your cat is cool, secure, and confident. She's the beautiful woman sitting at the end of the bar just knowing you'll buy her a drink. You want her to come running to greet you the minute you enter the door with her tongue wagging? Get a dog; it's just not happening.

You know what your cat needs from you? Food. They'd do it themselves and go hunt down some birds, but you seem willing to buy it and mix it up in a bowl shaped like their face, so knock yourself out. In return she'll walk by and rub against your leg once in a while. That makes you happy, doesn't it? You want her to do it on command? Good luck, just keep opening those cans.

You want them to sit on your lap more often? Now you're really getting desperate. Come on. Sure, your lap is warm but so is that spot on the floor by the dryer. Don't feel that your cat doesn't like you. She does; she just doesn't understand your kinky need to be sat on.

If I were a cat, I wouldn't just be aloof, I'd be downright afraid of people. I had a second-grade teacher named Mrs. Mayola who, for the most part, was a lovely person but whose obsession with cats bordered on psychotic. I guarantee that she liked cats more than her cats liked her. Every day she wore something with a cat on it and sat at her desk flanked by cat posters, writing with cat pencils that came from a pencil cup in the shape of a cat, with a handle shaped like a cat's tail. I never visited her home but I can only imagine that the first thing you'd see would be a giant door knocker in the shape of an American shorthair that was activated by pulling its tongue.

To other cat lovers she probably seemed pretty great, but if I were a cat I would figure out how to use the phone, contact the authorities, and report that a crazy person was obviously uncomfortably obsessed with me.

"Get over here, quick! You've got to see this place. She has, like, a thousand pictures of me all over the place. I have to hang up, I can hear her meowing in the hallway."

Cats don't have money or jobs or bank accounts, but if they did, the idea that they'd spend any of their hard-earned kitty income on refrigerator magnets, coffee mugs, and sweaters with human faces on them is absurd. It's not that they have anything against us; they just don't like us "in that way."

If you can't handle your cat's attitude, then maybe you're a dog person. Maybe you're one of those people who gets excited when their cat plays fetch or comes when they call. "He's just like a dog."

You've got the wrong pet. You never hear anyone excitedly tell you that their dog is just like a cat.

"The other day I gave Pepper a bone and he just scowled at me like he was expecting something nicer and walked off. He's just like a cat!"

My daughter tries to get our cat to play fetch. She'll toss some balled-up paper down the hallway, which will get the cat to chase after it, but as soon as he realizes he's been tricked into some sort of game, he walks on like he was heading that way all along. Dogs will fetch all day long. It's just not your cat's thing and, frankly, why is it yours? You throw something. They bring it back. How is this good for anyone?

Owning a cat is like dating a supermodel. It's going to be challenging, on her terms, and the more insecure you act, the more likely she'll run away. It's worth it but you're going to have to get it together and show a little self-respect. Stop begging for your cat's approval. Play hard to get once in a while. When you come home, walk right by her and go sit at the computer. Play it cool, maybe look at some dog websites, and before you know it she'll saunter across your desk and take a nap on your keyboard.

your dog doesn't want to go to a restaurant with you

I know it hurts. Every time you put on shoes and grab your keys your dog gives you those big sad "where are you going?" eyes, lowers his tail, and rips your heart out. With a single whimper he fills you with guilt and makes you question why you would choose a trip to the diner over dinner at home with your best friend.

"But, wait," you say, "restaurants are dog-friendly now! I'll just bring Mack along with me!"

Don't.

It's true, right there in the window of the restaurant is a cartoon dog with perky ears and a smile, giving you a thumbs-up. This seems perfect; you can bring him along and enjoy a guilt-free tuna sandwich. But the truth is the only thing your dog hates more than being left alone is going to a restaurant to watch you eat.

Look, no one likes to eat more than a dog. They love eating so much it doesn't even have to be food. They'll eat anything—bicycle helmets, remote controls, flip-flops. I once watched my sister's dog knock over and eat the entire contents of a garbage can, including the bag. And when he was done he looked up at me with pride in his eyes, threw it up, and ate that too.

So, why bring this eating machine to a place where he's the only one who's not allowed to eat? It would be one thing if they gave him a chair at the table, but he can't order, can't look at the menu, and the waiter won't even make eye contact with him. You drag him to this place and force him to sit there like the lonely guy with no money in a gentleman's club. Why are you doing this to him?

And the smells! A dog can smell a steak a mile away. He can smell the guy down the block opening a refrigerator. If there's a woman even thinking about making a beef stew later tonight, your dog is smelling it right now. Do you realize how many smells are pouring out of a restaurant? If your dog could answer he'd say, "A buttload."

When a dog is brought to a restaurant he must think it's some type of medieval obedience training.

"I didn't think he knew that I peed in the laundry basket, but he brought me to this steakhouse, tied me to his chair, and ate a New York strip right in front of my face! I've never seen him so mad!"

This doesn't mean that your dog is happy when you leave. He never gets used to it. He spends the first hour checking the window, then checking the door, then checking the window again, the door once more and, even then, he's not totally convinced you really left.

He loves you and he wants to know that you love him too. So show him, not by bringing him to the restaurant but by bringing the restaurant to him.

The doggy bag is a classic because it works. You go out, eat whatever you can, and the rest gets put into a bag and is given to your dog. Somewhere along the line people started eating from the doggy bags themselves. This is wrong. I'm not sure when this became acceptable, but it probably occurred around the same time that dogs started checking into hotels so they could be left in a strange room while their owners swam in the pool.

Everybody loves their dog and wants the best for them, but you have to really look at the situation and decide if you're doing it for the dog or yourself. I have a friend who is married, sleeps with his wife and two bullmastiffs. Two! That's about three hundred pounds of dog lying between him and his wife. He says that it's for the dogs, that they really need to sleep with him. Really? Or are you just excited, after twenty years of marriage, to have someone else to spoon with?

So don't torture your puppy. Leave him in the house with a treat, go stuff your face with nachos, and bring back what you can't finish. While you're at it, sneak him a little margarita on the side. Now that's a good friend.

get a fish

Every pet has its good points. They all bring their own unique brand of animal fun to the family, but the best advice I can give you is, get a fish. Getting a pet is a lot like getting a new boyfriend or girlfriend. Chances are you are going to get tired of them and when you do it's best that they live in a tank.

Fish are great. You always know where they are, you're never going to find a fish eating out of your garbage, and they don't jump up on the kitchen table and start licking the plates.

Fish don't lick at all. I've never seen a fish on its back licking its private parts like a candy cane and that's not only because I've never seen a fish tongue; I'm not even sure they have private parts. If they do, at least they have more class than my dog and would never mount another fish or start grinding on its castle and stare me down while they're doing it.

You don't worry as much about a fish. No one in the house ever panics and yells, "Where's the fish? Have you seen the fish? Oh my god, did the fish get out? He's going to attack the neighbors again!"

Fish don't get hit by cars, run away from home, or go missing in the middle of the night. You have never seen a flyer taped to a telephone pole with a close-up picture asking *Have you seen this fish?*

And they don't bother your guests. A fish isn't going to jump on the visitors to your home and run around their legs and pee at the same time. Do fish pee? Probably, but I know they don't pee on my guests in the hallway. They also won't grab a disgusting saliva-soaked stuffed toy and jam it into your guest's crotch until they agree to play tug-of-war with it. Fish don't fetch.

No one gets offended when someone brings their fish to a hotel, because they don't. And if they did, no one would know. I suppose you could smuggle them in in a jar, some crazy fish lover probably has, but who gets hurt?

They're clean too. Their tanks can get a little funky and grow green algae on the side, but you've got to love animals that you can wash with a sponge. Sure, a fish smells, but only when they come out of the water, and if they're out of the water they won't be around for long.

Do you know what a fish eats? Flakes. My dog eats flakes off the side of the dining room table because there's no amount of food that can satisfy her. We have to make a family trip to Costco, and two of us haul a fifty-pound bag of sweet potato-and-salmon-flavored food onto the cart, push it to the parking lot, load it into the car, drive it home, cut it open, put smaller amounts of it in jars, and in a week do it all over again.

The only thing my fish ever got from Costco was a bigger tank and a plastic skull he could swim through.

Fish don't beg. You only see one eye at a time. It's hard to beg with one eye. They don't shed. They don't drool. You don't have to walk them in the rain and the snow. They don't walk on the furniture. They don't climb on the table. You don't collect their feces in a box. They don't scratch your face. They don't stand at the end of the bed and stare at you when you're kissing your wife.

All they do is swim. All day. All night. To the peaceful hum of the filter. And when they die, it's a quick trip to the toilet and "goodbye."

Fish are the best.

good family pets

A Puppy
A Cat
Hermit Crabs
A Starfish
A Jell-O Mold
An Accountant
A Paper Clip
A Stuffed Squirrel
A Ball of Fuzz
A Personal Shopper

requiem for smokey

Our cat just died.

It's okay. We had three so, only two more to go. I'm kidding, *I'm kidding*. We only had two. I joke because it hurts when these pets, these furry family members, check out early. But I suppose it's all part of the deal.

You know when you bring them into your life that you're going to fall deeply in love, most likely outlive them, and they'll make you cry and swear to never go through that again. Until you find yourself walking past a pet adoption booth, outside the supermarket, and you look into a puppy's deep brown eyes and say, "Oh, what the hell."

My wife says that when our house is without a pet it feels dead. I guess my presence isn't the life-affirming gift that I thought it was, but I get what she means. That's why we're always cycling another animal through our system, with cats and dogs coming and going, fish being brought in one day and flushed out the next. The only pet we don't worry about is the gecko, who is expected to outlive all of us, which will be a funny day.

I picture the lizard, dressed in all black, composing himself as he greets guests at the funeral home.

"We're sorry for your loss."

"Thank you. They were an odd group of people, but really fun when you got to know them. I'll miss them, for sure, but, to be honest, I'm looking forward to the extra space."

I'm not as close to the pets as some of the people in my home are. I like them fine, but that's not really my role. As the father, it's my job to go out and get the pets, drive them home so the family can enjoy them, and when they reach the end of their life, I drive them back out.

I'm like the guy on death row who shows up for the final walk to the electric chair. The pets see me coming, cat carrier in hand, and they all back into their rooms and wonder who I'm coming for this time.

"I bet it's Reese. He's sure been walking funny," says the cat.

"Maybe it's just a visit to the vet for a checkup or something," says the fish.

"No way. We haven't seen this guy since the day Sneakers went missing."

A wise old cat playing his blues harmonica chimes in, "Don't pay him no mind. He'll be coming for all of us one day."

I don't enjoy this role, but that's life, as they say, and death, as I say, and my job, as my wife says.

Smokey, the latest cat I had to take to the vet, wasn't my favorite. We just never hit it off. I tried to hang out, I wiggled that feather thing on a stick, but she just didn't like me. We were like two roommates who tolerated each other but never went to the bar together.

At times she was downright mean. She had this habit,

whenever I walked into the room, of getting up on her hind paws, running full speed, and biting me on the leg. It should be noted that I never provoked her and not once did I ever do this to her. Not once. Yet, despite our awkward relationship, it was up to me to bring her to the vet when she got really sick.

I unzipped the case, she looked at me, looked around the vet's office, realized what was happening, and looked back at me.

"Really? You?" she asked.

"I know. I'm not feeling great about this, either," I replied.

The vet told me about the procedure. They were going to give her two shots. The first shot kind of calms them down, and then they administer the second shot, which is the closing scene. I nodded along, having heard this before, and told him that I understood.

And then in a hushed tone he said, "So, now we'll leave you two alone for a while so you can say your goodbyes."

Now, I didn't really need this extra time, but in the vet's office, in front of the vet and his misty-eyed assistant, I couldn't just say, "No, that's okay. I'm good. If you could just get that collar off, I'll sign whatever and get out of here."

So instead, I awkwardly reached out and pet her head.

"Thank you. I guess that would be best," I said.

The doctor nodded and looked down, the assistant started to cry; I tried not to laugh as I shut the door.

Now we're alone. I'm looking at the cat. The cat's looking at me. And I could swear she was trying to make me cry. As if she would only be satisfied if her last deed on this earth was to make me break down.

She looked up lovingly. She leaned into my hand as I

scratched behind her ear. But I stood strong. I wasn't going to cave in and let her have this final victory.

But then she started to purr.

It was her final purr. And I started thinking about how long that purr had been in our lives. How, for years, she had made the girls so happy, through birthdays and summers and holidays. And, in a few minutes, it was all coming to an end.

"You're not making me cry."

"Oh yes, I am," she said. And let out one last death purr.

Just as I broke down, and let out one of those blubbering burst of tears that only comes out when you're trying your best to hold it in, the vet opened the door.

"Oh, I'm so sorry. We can give you a little more time."

"No! We're good. Get in here, let's get going with the one-, two-shot thing."

Smokey leaned back and laughed.

The hardest part of losing one of our pets is watching my daughters have to deal with it. Seeing sadness, from the two people who I never want to have a sad moment, is tough to take. It's especially heartbreaking when they're doing their best to try to be brave.

It's an experience that even they have to go through, and it helps them to understand love, and loss, and courage. They learn that some goodbyes are forever and that a loved one can never be replaced.

Unless the loved one is a cat. In which case Dad runs out, finds a new kitten as fast as he can, and drives her home.

And the people rejoice.

bad family pets

A Worm
A Monitor Lizard
A Piñata
A Face-eating Monkey
A Baby
A Bowl of Fur
A Turtephan–Turtle Elephant Mix
A Little Person
A Walmart Greeter
A Lawyer

grandparents

Everybody loves the grandparents. If the grandparents in your family are your parents, they may not seem fun to you, but to anyone who calls them Grandma and Grandpa they are simply the best.

These elder statesmen walk into the room as survivors of decades of familial battles. They are the ones who beat the odds, raised their children, and are now living the good, small life. They may not have done any of it well, but they did it and for that they are beloved.

They no longer deal with major child-rearing issues or have to search for a bigger place with a more expensive mortgage and modern countertops. Theirs is a life made up of grandkids, free time, and errands. They'll walk to the post office to buy some stamps, send a card to their granddaughter, take a nap, and call it a day. Which it truly was.

When my grandparents came over it was like being visited by wacky wizards. They couldn't really see, or hear, or operate a coffeemaker, and yet they were able to hurl down the highway at high speeds and magically appear in our living room. They'd sit there with their impish smiles, holding secret satchels filled with things of wonder, just waiting to perform.

My grandfather wore little leather shoes, with white socks bunched up beneath his stretchy brown pants. He continually pulled his pants up so high that it looked like his waist started under his chin. He had to do this because they were so weighted down by all the stuff in his pockets. He had everything in there; all sorts of coins, pocketknives, ball bearings, maps, and lighters. He carried some fascinating stuff and could make a quarter appear from inside your ear, but he really couldn't compete with Grandma.

Grandma's magic was found in her mystical handbag. My nana would reach into her purse and magically conjure up anything we could dream of, as if she were one of Harry Potter's teachers. If you ever need to free yourself from jail, pick a lock, or just relax with a candy-coated honey stick, just ask Grandma.

Grandparents are funny, even if they're not trying to be. They walk funny, say things in a funny way, and are always trying to get a smile out of you. They're like the class clown who, just by staying around the school long enough, ended up becoming the principal.

Every grandparent has a little routine that they do, something special that they're known for. My grandfather's specialty was baseball. He was a lifelong Yankees fan, having been a child during the Lou Gehrig and Joe DiMaggio years. Regardless of the time of year, it seemed like the minute he would plop down on the couch, a game would instantly appear on the TV. He would tell long, detailed stories of Yankees history while watching the game and napping at the same time.

One of my grandmothers was the cook. She was permanently attached to the stove for days. She would come back from the store with nothing but an Italian bread and a block of Parmesan cheese and, like Jesus turning water into wine, she would create a meal for twenty or more people.

My other grandmother, Nana, was all about the games. Throughout my entire childhood, she carried a deck of cards up her sleeve like a dainty card shark, always looking for some action. She played it all, Go Fish, Kings in the Corner, and Bridge, and when she tired of those it was on to board games—Hangman and Tic-Tac-Toe. She was up for anything as long as it was play. Not work. Not school. Play.

That's a grandparent's greatest asset; that they don't have to take anything seriously anymore. Whatever problems might arise they aren't nearly as important as the time they can spend goofing around with their grandchildren.

Mine are all gone now and I miss them terribly. I miss their funny haircuts, their magic, and their greatest trick of all: making me feel like I was the most important person in the world.

fishing for sky

You can learn a lot from your grandparents. Little pearls of wisdom that only someone who has really lived can give you. For years my grandfather took me fishing, and, like all great nature stories, this one is filled with metaphors and deeper meanings and can be summed up in one sentence.

We never caught a single fish.

In the summers between the ages of ten and twelve he would pick me up early in the morning while the sun was just coming up over the horizon at the Jersey Shore. He would signal me by flashing his high beams when he pulled up because everyone else was still asleep.

Sneaking out of the house this early gave me the feeling that I was getting away with something, like we were partners in crime in one of those cop shows. He'd give me a wink from under his worn-out fishing cap, take a drag on his cigarette, hand me some gum, and we were off.

"Ooh boy!" he liked to say.

Our first stop was the bait shop, where we would buy a bunch of frozen squid and small fish with big eyes, encased in ice like dead Popsicles. "The smellier the better," my grandfather would say.

I liked the bait shop, or any shop that had such a singular purpose. You weren't going to find anything here but bait and the stuff to tie it to. I also liked the guy who ran the shop. He was old, grizzled, and scaly, as if he had just crawled out of the sea himself. He wore dirty overalls and looked like he never showered and why would he? He spent his life grabbing worms and fish with his hands and wiping them on his pants. Whenever he had a free hand he used it to take puffs of the ever-present cigar that hung from his lips. He was cool.

We would drive over the causeway, which was a bridge that connected Long Beach Island to the mainland, and once we arrived on the other side we'd park on the shoulder. This was back during a time when not enough people had been killed on the side of the road to give anyone the idea that there should be a law against it. Eventually they would.

We'd hop out of the car, gather our fishing poles and bait buckets, and try not to drop anything, while the pounding air from the tractor trailers roared passed us. We'd climb over the guardrail and down the small hill covered in uncut grass and trash that people would regularly toss out of their car windows.

Once we were under the bridge I was always surprised to see other people there. We would jockey for position among the other fishermen—an assortment of odd, shifty men who looked like they weren't here for fun, they were here for food. I don't remember anyone talking or having a particularly good time. I do remember trying not to get too close or make eye contact with them as we dropped our baited hooks into the water.

My grandmother always packed some sandwiches for us, and as was her trademark, she included a sliced pickle with it. I always liked this special touch. Something about those pickle slices made this frustrating adventure somewhat rewarding. My grandfather wouldn't eat his until we returned to the car because he was still convinced that someone had to man the poles in case a fish was about to bite. I knew better.

It always seemed like everyone caught fish but us. Everyone was pulling in nice-size bluefish and fluke, but the best we could do was snag some small, flat fish that was just dumb enough to be swimming by when we gave up and reeled in our lines. My grandfather would get angry, light another cigarette, and blame the bait, telling me to give the next piece a good squeeze so the guts would squish out a little.

This was the seventies, when "catch and release" wasn't yet a concept. People didn't care about their own health, so they definitely weren't thinking about the well-being of fish. Everyone kept whatever they caught, and if it was too small to eat they would chase each other around with it and stick it down each other's pants. These were the dumb years, around the time SeaWorld was just getting started.

When my grandfather finally got tired of not catching fish under the bridge, rather than admit defeat, we would pack up, head back over the bridge, and move to the ocean where we would try our luck with surf casting. This was a really stupid thing to do. Think about the size of the ocean—pick an ocean, any ocean. It's big, right? Now picture the size of a fishhook. One tiny fishhook. Now picture a ten-year-old boy, holding a fishing pole and trying with all his might to get that hook through the wind and into the ocean, from the beach. The best I could do was get it to land about three feet into the sea, smack in the middle of the crashing waves. The only time a fish is in that part of the ocean is when it's dead and being washed ashore. And that is where we fished.

For years.

We never caught a single fish.

Only one time did we try to go out into the water to where the fish actually were. We rented a little rowboat with a tiny motor but to us it was a yacht because normally my grandfather would never spend money on such a thing.

"Rich people go out on boats. We fish from under the road, like regular people."

I had gone to stay with my grandparents at their beach house. It was a little bungalow that they managed to buy, using up all of their money, forcing them to decorate the place with furniture they found in the garbage. Not coffee grinds and banana-peel garbage, but furniture that other people had left out on the curb. We would be driving down the street and my grandfather would scream out, "Card table!" We'd pull across three lanes of traffic before "some other lucky bastard gets there first." There wasn't a thing in that house that was paid for.

There were twelve chairs in the kitchen, no two were alike. The couch had no springs in it, "but how lucky are we that it matches the drapes!" The picnic table had a hole in it, the beds were broken, but it was beautiful because "it was all free." There was no air-conditioning, "but who needs that? We have the nice breeze from the ocean."

There was no shower inside but, "Isn't it great to shower outside with bright, blue sky? Just to be together and this close to the ocean is all we need! But keep your bathing suit on so that creep next door doesn't get a show."

The house sat across the street from a large water tower that stood several hundred feet high. The city painted it every couple of years and, in another example of living in a time when no one knew what they were doing, they didn't contain the paint with tarps and sheets as they do now. They would just blast it out with a spray gun and spray-paint the whole neighborhood. Homes, cats, and entire families walking with their beach chairs would be splattered.

In the way of an apology, the city would pay to have everyone's house repainted. This was a major inconvenience that my grandfather loved. "A free paint job! Ooh, boy!"

So when he said he was renting a boat it was a big deal. I was around twelve and had gone down to visit, along with my grandparents' friends Millie and John. All their friends from that World War II era were referred to as couples and had great couple names. Millie and John. Anita and Bob. Bill and Jewel. Viola and Arnold.

I was so excited to go out on a boat that the night before I prepared my rods, gathered my hooks and lures, and went to bed with a fishing magazine. John kept asking if I was on dope.

The boat my grandfather had rented was more like a canoe with an engine you would use to blend margaritas with. But, still, I was excited. Even though we weighed the boat down so much that water was coming in from the sides and we were the slowest thing on the bay, technically we were boating.

My grandparents and Millie and John got good and drunk on bottles of cheap beer, while I ran back and forth trying to fish. As boats passed us by John would point at me and yell, "You see this kid? He's on dope! Look at him. He's high as a kite."

They all had a good time but I wasn't there for laughs. I was there to finally catch a real fish off a real boat, like a real fisherman. But I didn't stand a chance. Fishing is hard enough without a bunch of old people throwing beer cans into the water and peeing off the side of the boat. Once again, the only thing I caught were pickle slices.

I went to bed that night in my crooked, used bed thinking, *Why do we do this, year after year, without ever catching a fish?* Was it our dedication to the fisherman's way of life? Was it our dedication to our roots as outdoorsmen?

No. We never caught a thing. Never.

We just liked standing next to each other for a couple hours and we needed some activity to let us do that. It would be weird if we just stood there.

My grandfather must have been thinking the same thing that night, and the next morning he finally admitted defeat. The fish had beaten us. He didn't come right out and say it, but rather than grab our fishing poles for another try, he reached into the closet and grabbed a kite.

"Let's give this a whirl," he said.

It's a very similar concept to fishing, really. You stand there, hold on to the end of a line, and chat away. But only this time, we started out having already caught something and we were letting it out little by little, but not so far that it wouldn't return.

He had this great trick of sending a message to the kite. He would take a small piece of paper and fold it around the extended, taut kite string and the wind would gently blow it

upward all the way to the kite. It had the great effect of con-
necting us there on the ground, to this thing that was flying
up above us.

"It's like fishing in the sky," he said. "Want to try?"

He handed me the line. The kite pulled and tugged in the
wind. It was up to me to hold on to it and keep it from blowing
away. I felt bigger and more in charge than I ever had in my
life.

"Okay, reel her in," he said.

As I wound the string and brought the kite closer to us I
told my grandfather that he was right, it was like fishing in
the sky. And for once we had actually caught something.

He lit another cigarette and smiled.

"Ooh, boy."

old people shouldn't twerk

There's a problem in this country. There's an epidemic that threatens to ruin the lives of millions of innocent people. And there's only one group who can stop it because they're the group doing it—the baby boomers.

Baby Boomers are senior citizens now. Those free-loving, original pot-smoking teens are now as old as a hippie's pair of Birkenstocks. But, apparently, no one has told them that. They still think they're at Woodstock. They're still partying, riding motorcycles, taking their clothes off in public, and running around like love-crazed teenagers, and it has to stop.

I get it if you want to do these things in the privacy of your own home, nursing or otherwise, but it's a different story if it's in the daylight, on the beach, among the young. It's great that you don't feel old, but this isn't about what you feel, it's about what we see.

Boomers have always had the conflicting reputation of being both selfish and community-minded, and it is to the latter part of their nature I make this appeal: We need you to act your age because we need old people.

We need traditional old people walking around in fishing

hats filled with hooks and lures. The kind of old people who wear warm jackets in the summer, long dresses at night, and little sweaters all year round. They play bingo and knit and bake cookies and tell stories about the good old days.

We don't need old people wearing backward baseball caps and yoga pants. We want grandmothers who are good at crafts not hanging out in bars, lining up Jell-O shots, and lifting up their shirts like someone trying to score beads at Mardi Gras.

We don't need old dudes taking over the gym either, showing up in sleeveless shirts and short shorts, flexing their muscles like a wrinkled Mr. Olympia. Why are they doing this? They can build up all the muscle in the world but they can't replace the skin on the outside. It's like chicken cutlets wrapped in Saran Wrap.

One of the culprits, of course, is the spread of erectile dysfunction pills. These devilish medications have not only extended parts of old men's physiques, they've done something far worse: They have extended adolescence. It's taken that insane time in a man's life when he can't stop thinking about girls and made it a lifelong condition. This isn't good.

If men are constantly chasing women, who will build the model airplanes and set up the train sets in the garage? Who will construct and paint our birdbaths? Who's going to sit in the park and smoke pipes and play chess? We need our grandfathers to talk to us about politics and baseball without distractedly glancing down at their phones to see if Sheila responded to the pic he just sent. It's not natural.

I would think that these poor grandmothers would be tired of being chased down by lecherous guys with walkers, but they seem to like it. If they didn't, they wouldn't be shooting

Botox into their faces and dressing in sweatpants with "Juicy" written on the bottom.

I hate to bring it up, but there has been a real spike in STDs in nursing homes, and this has nothing to do with the staff. All these residents are cruising down the hallways with their walkers, sneaking into each other's rooms, and turning "Heavenly Pines" into a frat house. The days are gone when your only worry was that grandma might catch a cold or pass out during Bingo.

The Boomers have even changed the concept of retirement. There was a time when the retired lived on a fixed income, maybe splurged on a carton of milk and a slice or two of bologna. This group is lined up at the bar at Dave & Buster's ordering appetizers and beers in a perpetual happy hour, flinging credit cards around and spending their children's inheritance gambling on Foosball.

And let me ask this: If they have so much energy and they are so "young," why aren't they working? There was a time when people retired, did some fishing for a couple years, and died. Today's group is retired for twenty, thirty years. That's a long time to be sending selfies from the poolside bar to your children while they're at work.

There are a lot of jobs that old people could do. It would be nice to see some old people bussing our tables and cutting our lawns. If you need some help fixing up the house, pull up to the nursing home, throw some old dudes in the back of the pickup truck, and enjoy some cheap labor. Why not? Forget drones and Amazon, put some old people on roller skates and send them out with the packages.

Seriously, though, we are struggling to figure out how to keep Social Security going, but the reality is we can't. Not if the millions of Baby Boomers continue to use it to fund their wife-swapping parties in Cabo.

Pretending to be young doesn't make you young. They can pretend all they want, but they can't feel that great. I'm in my forties and I'm already starting to creak. In the morning, as I hobble off to the bathroom, I feel like I'm walking on tin-can ankles. You would think that I had been running a marathon, not sleeping for eight hours in a comfy bed.

What's really upsetting is how aging affects everything on your head. Your eyes go, your hearing is shot, your taste buds are different. Your nose seems to work but not like it used to or old people would realize they don't smell that great.

This isn't fair at all. I could deal with a cranky knee, but when you can no longer read the menu or hear your friend talking because you're in a bar that's playing music in dim lighting, it's pretty depressing, and time to start hanging out somewhere else.

I'm not saying to quit living your life, just do the job we need you to do. We need you to show young people that the dumb part of their life will one day come to an end and they can look forward to living with dignity and poise.

You're not fooling anyone and, even worse, you're scaring the children.

perfect gift ideas for grandma

Anything with your name on it
Anything with your picture on it
Something that you made
A piece of paper with a spray-painted noodle on it
Anything with a flower on it
A poem that you wrote
A song that you sing
Something with your hair glued to it
Yarn
A bottle of whiskey

who's watching who?

Many parents are so desperate to get away from their families that they participate in the wildly irresponsible act of leaving their children with their parents. It is a false sense of security, because your parents are only slightly more responsible than the children and are likely much less competent. When you get in that car, hit the horn, and wave goodbye, ask yourself one question: "Who's watching who?"

I am far more worried about leaving my parents alone in my house than my children. They're a wreck. My kids won't open a jar of tomato sauce, pour it into a pot, and let it boil, without stirring it, until it bubbles and splatters all over the kitchen, but my mother will. My children won't order a mini power washer and wander around the house "cleaning" every surface until the paint chips off and then declare that it feels much better this way.

The kids won't take my car out to a restaurant, yell at the kid working the parking valet that it's too expensive, screech off in a huff and "show him" by parking on a side street without reading the parking sign that clearly reads NO PARKING

WITHOUT PERMIT and leave me with a sixty-dollar ticket, like my father did.

How do I know all of these misdeeds? Because the kids tell on their grandparents. It's like having two living, breathing nanny cams recording everything. I'm starting to feel that we're better off not hearing about it.

When the dog peed on the floor and my parents couldn't be bothered with cleaning it up, they just tossed a page from the sports section at it. It sat there for several days and was only picked up five minutes before I walked back in the door. At least that's what the kids put down in the report.

They also keep a running total of all the times their grandfather curses, which is quite a lot, and pretty much at everybody, including their grandmother. He curses so much and so colorfully that the kids don't even recognize some of the words he comes up with. To make them feel better I told them that he used to be a pirate.

When the kids are small, you never hear about the life-risking mistakes your parents are making and that's probably better. You just want to come home and find that everyone is still alive. You may see clues, some smeared peanut butter on someone's face, maybe a beer bottle under the coffee table, but you don't ask any questions. You got out of the house, had a good time, and no one is in the emergency room. That's really all you want.

So why do I get nervous when my parents, who helped me survive, are now watching my children? Because they're older now, not very focused, and they take a lot of naps. If something went wrong and my father had to wake up and run out of the house to drive the kids to safety, there's a good chance his car would be gone, because he parked it in a tow-away zone. He'd spin around trying to find it and forget why he came outside in the first place, go back inside, lay down, and take another hap.

Beyond their lack of skills, there is also a lack of urgency to their job. My parents' attitude is that they're watching my kids, not raising them. They already went through all that worrying and trying to do the right thing. Now they're just trying to enjoy the weekend while these kids are around.

"You want to make s'mores on the stove and stay up to watch *Saturday Night Live*? Does your mother let you do that?"

"Umm . . ."

"Ah, what the hell, have fun, I'm going to bed."

What do your parents care if the kids don't sleep for 48 hours, get sick, and their week is ruined? By the time that happens they'll be long gone.

There's nothing better than leaving for a couple of days and knowing that your children are being cared for. However, if you've left them with the old people, don't be lulled into thinking that it's a great level of care. In a lot of ways, you'd probably be better off if the dog was in charge. Come to think of it, he probably is.

bad gift ideas for grandma

Yoga Pants
UFC Fantasy Camp
Afro Wig
A robe that is difficult to keep closed
Trampoline
Fracking Equipment
Nipple Tassels
Jawbreakers
Tickets
Contraception
LSD

the outlaws

When you marry someone, hopefully it's because you love them. You decided that they are the one person who you could spend the rest of your life with. What we seldom consider is that they come with a whole bunch of other people who you did not approve of but who will now be in your life forever.

And the most dangerously invasive of all these new relatives is their parents.

Your spouse has a relationship with these people. A lifelong relationship that may be great, may be terrible, but, either way, you are a fool to get involved. You cannot honestly express your feelings about these people. It is not your place. You must remember that you are there to support your spouse, not comment on her parents, regardless of how awful they may be.

Even when your spouse goes on a tirade about them, just nod your head and don't say a word. Take the same approach when one of your friends breaks up with their boyfriend/girlfriend. You might feel free to finally attack them and say everything you've always wanted to say, but keep in mind there's a real good chance they'll get back together and you'll have to sit across from them at dinner.

So I won't comment on my in-laws, I'm not that dumb. Especially in a book that will forever be on some shelf somewhere as long as there are shelves and, God willing, books. And I'm not just avoiding the bad things—and there are bad things, horrible things—but also the good.

I will not thank them for successfully raising their beautiful daughter who ultimately became my wife. I wasn't around when she lived at home with them, and as difficult as it is for me to believe, they somehow got past their psychotic behavior and raised her into a beautiful, thoughtful woman. I don't ask how.

If I were to thank them for that, then it would be intellectually unfair to not include all the negative things that I have seen, in the time that I have been around. And why would I want to do that, to point out their shortcomings? That's not nice.

Why would I spend time exposing all their selfish, self-obsessed attitudes, when I have to continue to see them? That wouldn't be smart. Wouldn't that just make them crankier than they normally are? Wouldn't that make them torture my wife with more inane, guilt-filled phone calls? No. I refuse.

I won't attack these two people who try to belittle everyone in their family, without ever looking in the mirror and trying to fix the failures in their own lives. I'm no dummy.

I made a promise on our wedding day to protect my wife, but sometimes it is best to protect the ones you love by quietly keeping things to oneself until I can mock them onstage and hope that no one is recording it.

It's better that I just live my life and not get involved.

That being said . . .

your father-in-law
doesn't like you either

We don't like to be judged. We didn't like it on the play-ground, don't like it at work, and don't like it from our par-ents. We spend a lot of time mitigating the effects of what they think of us, and just when we finally reach a point when we are done caring, we marry into an entirely new family. Suddenly we have an entire new group of people judging and evaluating us all over again, and they have a lot of catching up to do.

If you're a man, no one is going to judge you more harshly than a father-in-law. The minute you show up this man hates you. There's no way around it. He may act cordial, he might shake your hand, ask you to go hunting, but deep inside he wants you dead.

He knows what you're up to. He knows what you're doing. He knows what you're thinking. None of it's good and it's all with his daughter.

Do you realize what a father has to do, mentally, to not kill you the minute you walk in the door? It's instinct. I know it's a cliché, the angry dad bringing out a shotgun when he meets his daughter's boyfriend, but allow me this. Clichés stick around because they carry so much truth that we can't help but repeat them over and over and make bumper stickers, T-shirts, and corny elevator jokes out of them.

You can't blame a bunch of fathers for not articulating this deep feeling in some new creative fashion just to avoid sounding like every father who came before him. He's not trying to be clever. He just wants you dead.

I watched my father deal with my sisters' boyfriends. It was not good. In his mind his daughters were too tripped up by hormones and emotions to think straight. It was up to him to do the practical work that my sisters were powerless to do: destroy every boy who came to the house and make them go away.

He would start with a handshake. He's a big handshake, eye-contact guy. Looking someone in the eye was very important to him. It was important because he had scary eyes and any kid who looked into them would immediately feel intimidated and start to cry. And he liked this.

His handshake was tough. He had the grip of a polar bear reinforced with hydraulics. There are a lot of guys like that out there. You run into them all the time. You say, "Hello, nice to meet you," and out of nowhere they crush your hand like it's an empty Coke can.

If you're not ready for it, there's very little you can do.

You weren't anticipating being in a contest, you were just being nice at this cocktail party, didn't come in hard enough, and now this guy is holding your fingers like you're a French queen. "Oh, we're doing this now? Really?" All you can do is submit and be judged as a lesser man than him. This sounds primitive, and it is, and it sounds like it shouldn't matter, but it does.

Now you can imagine the advantage my father had over the teenagers who came calling at the house. Even if they were ready for it, and they were not, they didn't stand a chance against his giant, angry-man hands. And to add some extra spice to it, my father would not only squeeze their hand but start squishing it around like an old dishrag. He applied squeezing, pulsing, bone-crushing shakes that immediately brought tears to their eyes. He thought this was hilarious. He truly did. This was how he had fun. In a world of unjust pecking orders and disproportionate wealth, his handshake was the great equalizer.

My friends would ring the doorbell, jump off the porch, and wait in the middle of the yard while he answered the door.

"Is Tom home?"

"Get over here and say hello," my father would say.

"No."

"Come on, don't be a wimp."

"No, I'm good."

"Now."

They couldn't fight it. An adult was making them do something, so they would come over, put out their hands, and he would crush their hands, make them fall to their knees, and laugh. Eventually most of them laughed too. It's what he was known for.

Sometimes he would take it too far. He saw it as a test of a kid's character, but sometimes he met new kids and their character wasn't that great. Or maybe they were just a little frightened of the world. Now this big man, who they don't know, was coming up to them at this brunch, and was squeezing their hand until they cried. Some really cried. Like, cried out for help to the point that their parents and all the other parents would come running into the room and find the kid on the ground and my father giggling.

"You've got to toughen this kid up."

My mother was extremely embarrassed. She would apologize and make excuses for him. "He gets carried away. Apologize, Tom."

"Okay. I'm sorry. Let's shake on it."

And it happened all over again.

"That kid's not going to last," he'd say on his way to the buffet.

So along comes a boy who likes my sister and wants to make a good impression. He comes to meet my father, and my sister sits there nervously, knowing what's about to happen. I would say only about 2 percent of the guys got past the front door. The kid would leave disgraced with a hurt hand and my sister would run up to her room. My mother would scream and my father would go back to watching the game without a flicker of a second thought that maybe this was the wrong approach.

Was it? All he was doing was expressing the very real feelings that every dad has. He wasn't hiding it. He wasn't keeping it inside. He was out to destroy these hormonal, acne-faced invaders, one by one, unless they passed his test.

My one sister was sixteen when she started dating a long-haired, not very athletic senior. I didn't think he stood a chance but for some reason the handshake had no effect on him, he just laughed. He was probably high. He entered the house as if my father wasn't even there. Knowing this might never happen again, she married him and they are still together to this day.

When you are the young man calling on the daughter,

you see her father as just a guy who stands in your way. You've fallen for this girl and suddenly there's this old goofball in a baseball cap trying to stop you. You want to take him out but you can't attack him, on account of the whole lifelong history thing they have going.

Knowing that brute force isn't going to work you have to apply a little son-in-law jujitsu. You have to respectfully stand your ground, absorb his flailing blows, and wait until he runs out of gas. When his punches are no longer a threat you thank him kindly and escort his daughter out of the house.

It's a battle as old as the hills and I find myself on the other side of it now, as I stand ready to protect my daughters at all cost. Recently this kid came around, and from the minute I saw him talking to my girl, I wanted to punch him. I could tell that this little eight-year-old con artist had just one thing on his dirty little mind. So I sat in the back of the bowling alley for the entire birthday party just waiting for my chance to knock him out.

My daughter politely asked me to leave.

best places to bring your daughter's boyfriend

A Shooting Range
A Boxing Gym
A Church
An Empty Room
A Cemetery
Your Friend Julio's Apartment
A Boat Out at Sea
A Tent in the Woods
A Mafia-Run Steam Room
The Bronx
Rikers Island State Prison

your mom's not
the boss of me

Many people feel enormous pressure to make their in-laws happy, and will do whatever it takes in order to win their approval. They will change their habits, eat foods they detest, and edit what they say in order to not cause waves.

My wife is not one of those people.

She loves my parents, and my parents love her, but initially mixing them together was like adding a drop of vinegar to a bowl of oil. I take full responsibility. My parents are good people but they come from a different time and place, and simply weren't ready for her. I should have given them a little warning so they could've prepared themselves and been more careful about saying the wrong things. I assumed they were more progressive but, as it turned out, I blindsided them and, without any warning, I brought home—a vegetarian.

My wife stopped eating meat when, as a teenager, she connected in her mind that meat came from animals. She really likes animals, considers them her friends, and this realization made her extremely uncomfortable. She decided to never eat meat again. Conversely, my family has been eating animals forever. A lot of animals. Sure, they consider one or two of them to be their friends, but the rest they see as the course that comes right after the pasta.

The thing about an Italian family is that eating is a way of bonding with each other. The sharing of food, or rather the force-feeding of food, is the way that you show your love. An Italian mother greets you by telling you that you're hungry.

"Mom, meet Cindy."

"Nice to meet you. You look hungry. I'll get you something to eat."

This was the loving way that my mother welcomed my wife-to-be. It was a sweet introduction that went well until my mother brought out a plate of meatballs, pasta with meat sauce, sausages, pepperoni, chicken parmigiana, and prosciutto with melon. And this was all before the meal even started.

My wife looked at the food, looked up at my mother, and said, with unflinching confidence, "Thank you, but I don't eat meat."

Have you ever been smacked in the face? It hurts, but even more than that, you're stunned. There is a moment when you don't realize what is happening. You freeze. Your eyes go crossed. Reality is turned on its head and you reach out for something to take hold of while you try to make sense of what just happened. That's how my mother felt when my wife delivered this news.

"I'm sorry, what did you say?"

"I don't eat meat."

Someone dropped a plate.

This is like telling a lifelong democrat that you voted for Trump. It's like telling a Red Sox fan that you love the Yankees. She may as well have said, "I'm not really into this whole Italian thing that you've got going on."

At first my parents didn't even know what it meant.

"You mean you don't eat steak, but you'll have meat sauce?" asked my mother.

"No, no meat," my wife replied.

"But you'll eat meatballs."

"No."

"So you just want the sauce from the meat sauce?"

"It can't be made with meat."

"Just a little meat?"

"No meat."

"Chicken?"

"No."

"Pork?"

"No."

"Bacon?"

"No meat."

"Well, how do we make the sauce with no meat?!"

"I don't know."

"Jesus, Mary, and Joseph! Tommy, what have you done?!"

My father eats sheep heads. He eats the eyes out of fish. He is a monster. He has a drawer filled with T-shirts that he won as part of meat-eating contests. He stops at White Castle for a dozen burgers on his way to a steak house. He looked at me and rolled his eyes, as if I, too, was hearing this for the first time.

I'm a bit of a chameleon. I'll change, adapt, and make stuff up just to avoid any tension. Maybe it's the performer in me, but I aim to please. My wife aims to kill. Not out of ill will or a desire to hurt, but she is going to stick to her position no matter what. I think it's called a belief system. When I'm uncomfortable, the only thing I believe is that I should be going.

My wife held her ground despite many meals and even more comments. Seeing that she wasn't going anywhere, my parents tried to bend the rules any way they could. My mother scraped tomato sauce off the top of the meat sauce. My father put a plate of salami near her, as if that would tempt her into seeing clearly. They would lie about the ingredients of dishes.

"No, there's no meat in that lamb chop."

"It's made with lamb."

"Is it?"

And they didn't even consider mentioning chicken stock, fish, or shrimp because, "Come on, those don't count."

It's a battle that continues to this day. Now that my kids are vegetarians, as well, my mother tries even harder. "How are they going to get their protein? They need protein. Here, kids, take this hot dog with you, put it in your pocket, don't tell your mother."

To her credit, my wife didn't fight them or get annoyed. She was used to people's confusion and frustration about the way she ate. She just smiled and ate the salad, in-laws be damned.

However, my wife did not prevail in the battle with my parents over her privacy. She grew up in a family that had things like alone time, short visits, and separate vacations. She married into a family that has none of that. My family has no secrets. Zero. That's a nice way of saying that everyone is constantly in everyone else's business.

"Get over here. Tell us everything. Why haven't you called? Where have you been? We haven't spoken to you since lunchtime!"

This was a shock to my wife's system. She was just getting to know me and now she had a houseful of crazy people interrogating her. Her family didn't ask each other intimate questions at all, let alone scream at them across a crowded dinner table.

"How long have you been sleeping with my son? Is your father an alcoholic? What kind of name is that? What are you, Polish or something?"

She was shell-shocked. Her family didn't even celebrate holidays. Not for religious reasons; they just didn't see the point. My parents asked them to come over on Thanksgiving and Christmas, ten years in a row. They declined every time.

"But we're family!" my parents would yell with a mouthful of spaghetti.

Their silent response was, "No, we're not."

Don't get me wrong, this made the holidays very simple for my wife and I. We avoided all the complications and endless driving between family celebrations. It was one stop at my parents' house for Christmas and then we'd see her family at a diner on some random Tuesday when they were nearby doing something else.

But for all the convenience, my parents didn't like this at all and decided they had to double down on the family events, insisting we get together for every holiday, birthday, and any other reason they could come up with. They saw it as their duty to show my wife that they really, really loved her by pulling her in closer and learning every detail of what she was thinking.

At first my wife tried to get out of it. She would come up with what she thought were clever excuses, but when it's one person against an entire family she stood little chance. And once we created grandchildren for them, as the Jersey Italians say, "Fuggedaboutit."

So she goes, and with each year she seems to enjoy it more and more. She has come to accept this incredibly intrusive amount of togetherness and their relationship works. But no matter how many times they tell her that a meatball doesn't have meat in it, she knows better.

brothers & sisters

You show up in a home, as an infant, straight from the maternity ward and there are these big people who seem to be in charge of everything. But as you look down low, there are also some shorter people stumbling around, who seem to be in the same position as you. They're small, make a lot of noise, and apparently have no power. These are your siblings and, even though they've already hit you and you don't like the way they wear their diapers, you realize that forming an alliance with them is probably a good idea.

Who else will help you to convince your parents that you really need a dog or that a trip to Disney is crucial for your well-being? If you sneak out of your room, who is going to be on lookout? There's Halloween candy that needs to be smuggled into your bed, wrappers to be hidden, and it's all at least a two-man job.

They are a constant part of your life. There will be the inevitable highs and lows, closeness and distance, but till the end of time, when someone asks if you have brothers or sisters you'll answer yes.

There will always be a bond, like old army buddies who

survived a war together. They were with you in the trenches, during the good times and bad. They are the people who you ran down the stairs with on Christmas morning, helped you blow out the candles on every cake, and who saw you cry in your room as you licked your wounds.

Together, you learn to count the stars and figure out what those clouds looked like and how to fall asleep when you're scared. You build forts and hide under blankets from the thunder and have uncontrollable laughing fits and cry together when death intrudes on your lives for the first time.

But a sibling is also a competitor. This is the first person who you will compare yourself to and the first example that everything is unfair. "Why do they get to do that, eat that, stay up later, have a sleepover?" "They have more candy than I do." "How come she gets to sit in that chair that I didn't know I wanted until she sat in it?"

They were the person who you first tried everything out on, who showed how loving and how surprisingly mean you could be. One minute you're pals, the next you're yelling at them to get out of your room. Sisters are awful and icky. Brothers are gross and dumb.

My friend and I stuck my one sister in a garbage can. When crabs were biting my other sister's feet in the bay and she was crying for help, rather than lend her a hand I sat on the dock and laughed. Both times they looked at me shocked that I could turn on them like that, and I was a little shocked too, and the fact that I'm writing about it now shows that I still carry the regret. But growing up is an ugly endeavor at times and we can only try to be good when we know how awful it feels to be bad.

They are a part of your life forever. Friends will come

and go, but your sister will always be your sister and your brother will always be on your mind. You can call every day or not talk for years, but they are always there, as someone you send a card to, or tell a horrible story about to a stranger in a bar.

We're just people and, although we come from the same family, we navigate through life in different ways, with different outlooks and different tools. Like classmates graduating from the same high school, everyone comes out having had vastly different experiences and in the end we all go our own way. Your brother could end up living in New Mexico on a cactus farm while your sister takes the subway to work every day in midtown Manhattan.

Regardless of how great, or strained, or nonexistent your relationship with your sibling is, it is unavoidably bittersweet. This was the first little hand that reached out to take hold of yours and let you know that you were loved. The squeeze of their fingers told you that things were going to be okay. That you were not alone. There's no way to maintain or regain that profound closeness ever again and with that comes a natural pang of regret. Should we have stayed closer? Could we have done more?

And what the hell happened back there?

mistake in the woods

If you're married and your spouse has a crazy brother named Jerry who has a drinking problem with a temper to match and he invites you to go camping in New Jersey, just say no. I said yes, and it was the most miserable twenty-four hours of my life.

The mistake I made was going along with his idea when he brought it up the first time. When you hang out with a guy who drinks like it's a contest, and he's "family," there is a good chance that you will drink too. You may not drink an entire liter of cheap scotch that comes in a bottle with a handle on it like he does, but you'll definitely drink more than you should. Enough that when he brings up the idea that "We should all totally go camping together!" you find yourself, against everything you believe, giving him a high five.

"Yes! We are totally doing this!" he said, and went back to stabbing his knife into the table around my hand.

When you say "yes" to an alcoholic you are at his mercy because, as a drunk, he doesn't differentiate between a drunken plan and a sober plan. To him they're just plans. So once you agree, you essentially jump into a roaring river of drunk with him, and all you can do is hold on to the sides of the boat and try not to be flung into the water.

Why does a drunk from South Jersey want to go camping? It's not to hike. It's not to go rafting or check off species in his bird-watching book. It's to drink in the woods. That's it.

Think about it, where do you camp in New Jersey? I'm sure if you go to the official New Jersey website there are a lot of links to lovely trails and state parks that try to con you into believing that Jersey is just as wonderful a camping destination as the Rocky Mountains. Don't believe it.

I grew up in New Jersey, and I know there are some of you Jersey folk who are screaming in protest right now, but let's not confuse pride with reality. I love Jersey. I truly do. It's much more beautiful and diverse than people are led to believe when they enter the state through the grimy underbelly of Newark Airport.

But if you think that camping in New Jersey is a good idea, you're delusional. There are no mountains, there are hills. There are no rivers, there are creeks. There are no national parks, there are state parks with reservoirs, where old people walk their dogs and drug dealers set up shop.

There are campgrounds, but that's a loosely defined term in Jersey. They're really just places to sleep on the side of the road. This might be for the night in a tent, in a car for an hour or two, or perhaps, long-term in a trailer or motor home. The "campground" that my alcoholic brother-in-law chose for our weekend getaway was a place where people did all three.

It was a steaming hot, deep August, Jersey day. The kind of hot that knees you in the crotch when you open the door. The kind of hot that pins you to the ground and sits on your

face in its underwear and doesn't let you up until you say
uncle, which you can't do because there's a hot crotch in your
face.

We should have canceled. It was unsafe to be outside in
this heat. The news said the air wasn't breathable. It was the
kind of heat that stopped you from thinking and spun you
around in circles. Parades were canceled. Water parks shut
down. When the fire department got calls they let them go
to voice mail because they knew the fires would just make
them hotter.

But my wife and I did not cancel. We couldn't disappoint
her brother and let him drink in the forest by himself, so we
got in our car and drove. The car bucked and hesitated like a
horse that'd been spooked by danger up ahead. Smoke came
out of the hood, the steering wheel was hot to the touch, and
the air-conditioning was too tired to get out of bed.

We pulled up to the campground, but at first glance it
looked a lot like a trailer park. It had trailers, like a trailer park.
It had stray dogs chasing naked children around, like a trailer
park. This really seemed like a trailer park.

"Is this a trailer park?" we asked the man at the main en-
trance who was chewing on a stick.

"Yep," he replied.

"Oh, sorry, we thought it was a campground."

"People camp over theres," he said, as he pointed over
theres.

"Oh," said I.

As our car reluctantly creeped over theres, I kept hoping it
was a mistake. Or, at least, that we arrived first and I could
speed off and call them once we got home and say, "We got

lost and ended up in a trailer park, totally weird. You probably got lost too. Maybe next time."

But I wasn't that lucky. Not only had he gotten there before us but he got there with enough time to set up camp, which meant he opened the trunk of their car, pulled out some wood, and built a bar. I'm not kidding. A full-service bar. Two shelves with more than twenty bottles displayed as if it were the White Horse Tavern. This was going to be trouble.

Jerry stood proudly next to it as we got out of the car. He was wearing the official "drinking in the woods" uniform: jean shorts, no shirt, with a bandanna tied around his head. He had a crazy look in his eye and was pouring sweat.

"I didn't know what we'd be drinking so I brought it all!"

His wife was complimenting him and his craziness in hopes that he would pass out before he started swearing at her and knocking her around.

I didn't know what to say. I was already dizzy from the heat and becoming nervous because I was starting to see things.

"If you're staring at my chest and think I have three nipples, I don't. That third one is just a birthmark. Looks like the start of a nipple but it ain't got the juice," he said as I gagged.

When I'm in a situation like this, a bad situation, when I am unhappy with what's going on, I tell myself not to say anything and then say it anyway. I can't help it. I say it so many times in my head that it just pops out of my mouth.

"We've got to get out of here. Someone's going to die!"

"Ha, ha. No way, I've got us covered," he said. "There's a swimming hole but it's about a mile from here so, in the meantime, I made this."

He pulled out a white bucket, the kind they use on con-struction sites to haul tools and fill with cement and nails, only now it was filled with water. "You sit on a bench, put your feet in the bucket, and it cools off your whole body. It's just like air-conditioning," he said.

It was not.

"Feet don't fit in no bucket," I said to myself, slowly turn-ing into a hillbilly. They really don't. To get them in, you have to point your toes like you're wearing high heels. This wasn't going to cool us down. This was something you would only do if your feet were on fire. If you were at a Tony Robbins semi-nar and tried to walk across hot coals and your feet caught fire just like you knew they would, only then would you use this dumb bucket.

My wife and her sister-in-law were off chatting and I just stood there watching Jerry making a Long Island Iced Tea, feeling anxious and trapped. We obviously weren't going to get out of there and the temperature was well over a hundred, with the legendary New Jersey humidity, that kills a whole bunch of old people each year, wrapping around us like a wool sweater.

I decided to seek relief and stumbled into a wooden shower stall, filled with spiders, beer cans, and a dirty pair of men's white underwear. I didn't care, I needed some cold water on my body, but the pipes were so hot that when I turned the faucet, it just spat out steam. I almost started to cry.

When I came stumbling back and saw Jerry already drunk, shooting squirrels with a BB gun, I made the irratio-nal decision to head to the swimming hole. The only expla-nation I can give for thinking that jumping into what was probably the runoff of all the toilets in this godforsaken trailer park is that I was desperate, confused, and might have been having a stroke.

Jerry liked the idea and the two of us started walking down a dirt path together. I had stripped down to my shorts and poured the foot bucket on my head, so now we looked like two members of the Village People after a show.

"Swimming hole" was the proper name. It was a hole. The kind they put the word "hell" in front of. It was a disgusting brown semblance of a small lake. A pond, really. A place where a local chemical plant would dump their toxic waste without thinking they'd done anything wrong and the locals would shrug their shoulders like they expected as much.

There were people in it. People who obviously thought this was a good idea. They must have been just as hot and desperate as I was because they didn't seem to notice the layer of film on the top. A greenish-orange layer of bubbly fermented crust that clung to their bathing suits and coated their children's faces as they doggy-paddled across the surface.

I don't like to swim in hotel pools because they're not clean enough. I'll skip a bath in my own tub if I suspect it hasn't been scrubbed. But I went in. Willingly. There was no jumping in, so I had to wade in slowly as my feet sank into the gelatinous goo that sat at the bottom.

"It's even hot in here," said Jerry.

He was right. There was no relief. I was submerged in a noxious soup, surrounded by mutant sea monkeys, and I swear I was hotter than before I got in.

There was nothing left to do but drink.

I know you shouldn't drink alcohol in the sun, but what

else could I do? I sat with my feet in a bucket, with a brown film covering my body, and drank everything Jerry gave me. I even ate the Hormel Chili, that he said didn't really need to be heated up, right from the can. Some of it spilled into my foot-bucket water but I didn't care. I got drunker and drunker, to the point where I was staring right into the sun, trying to make it go down with my eyes, which it eventually did.

As soon as it was dark we stumbled into our tent and lay down on top of the hard ground praying for God to knock us out. I was almost asleep when a car roared straight for us across the gravel parking lot. Screaming, I grabbed my wife and waited to be run over, thinking God had answered my prayers.

The car suddenly stopped not five feet from our bed. Headlights shone in our faces as the car doors opened and people got out. With a drunk, shaky hand I unzipped the tent, looked out, and saw a family, a fat family of five, carrying balloons and a cake, making their way to one of the trailers for a birthday party.

Although I still have moments of arrogance and can be judgmental of people, I will never mock people who live in a trailer park again. How can I? I slept in their driveway. These people must have looked at me, lying there, dirty, filled with booze and covered with deer ticks and thought, *Look at this degenerate. What a waste of a life.*

I never said goodbye to Jerry. I never even packed up my tent. We woke up before the sun and realized I wasn't drunk. I had sweat everything out in my sleep. We quietly got in the car and sped out of that place as fast as we could, leaving the tent, sleeping bags, and a little piece of our souls behind.

So don't make the same mistake I did. I don't care if they're a brother, sister, or even a parent. If they start making drunken plans that sound like trouble, don't humor them with "yeahs" and "maybes." Just say no.

the brother i never had

I never had a brother. As much as I loved my sisters, I was always aware that there wasn't a brother around. It wasn't something I complained about, or said out loud, but it was a secret wish of mine. The closest I got was when I moved to a new town and met my friend Keith. He was as much a brother to me as anyone would ever be. But it didn't last.

I came into a new school in early October. This was an especially intimidating time to move, as the school year was already a month old, friend groups were set, and on this day, class had already begun.

After an awkward introduction by the teacher I found a spot on the floor right next to Keith. I must have been wide eyed and scared because that was the first thing he teased me about. He bugged his eyes out of his head, laughing at me with his friends. I was intimidated and frightened, but I also knew they were being funny, so I returned the bug-eyed look and he laughed and we quickly became friends. Sometimes that's all it takes when you're young.

Keith was short with fair Irish skin, freckles, and reddish-brown hair. He had a mischievous look about him, like those troublemaking, streetwise kids from the old movies on Turner Classic. But whatever wariness people had about him was quickly dispelled by the smile that took over his entire face. And he was always smiling.

He was simply the funniest person I've ever known. I attribute his sense of humor to his large Irish family. They were the kind of family where everyone was funny. The parents, his six sisters, brothers, everyone was quick and sarcastic and ruthless. You couldn't survive around them without a good sense of humor. They didn't say hello, they teased you about your haircut and waited for your comeback.

Although they were basic Irish Catholics there was something WASPish about how they lived. They had a built-in bar in their basement. They drove expensive but practical cars. They golfed and belonged to a country club. They let us stay up late to watch the *Tonight Show with Johnny Carson* who seemed to be a role model to them all. They seemed to have everything in order. I liked it there.

Keith was really small in size but was a really big wiseass. This led to trouble. He couldn't always physically match up to the other kids but he was so funny he could destroy anyone with a single sentence. For years he would mock the bigger kids, they would get mad, he'd mock them more, and then they'd beat him up. When I arrived, as unusually big as he was small, that all stopped. I spent the next six years punching anyone who got near him.

I never had a brother and now I did. We understood each other as only brothers can. We were together all the time. In a way we were closer than actual brothers. We weren't fighting for a spot in our families like we were with our real siblings.

We didn't have the battles that real brothers had. We just had fun on our endless mission to make each other laugh.

We played football and climbed onto the roof of the school on Sundays, retrieving the tennis balls and Frisbees that got stuck up there during the week. We ran through the woods, lay on our backs in a giant open field, looking up at the sky without needing to understand how rare this free time was. We had no money. No commitments. No jobs.

We raced through childhood together. Nearly every day for six years was spent together. Six years between the ages of eight and thirteen is a lifetime. We grew together, changed together, found our way together. We discovered music and comedy together. Played albums over and over and recited every funny line from *Airplane!* and *Love at First Bite* and *Saturday Night Live*.

We were living in a vast accumulation of space that we actually felt as we slept at each other's homes through nights of endless laughter, driving our parents insane because we wouldn't go to sleep. But we really couldn't. The pool of things that would make us laugh was endless and turning out the lights seemed to make it wash all over us. Snickers turned into laughter, which made our parents yell, which made us laugh harder until we were forced to bury our faces in tear-covered pillows.

For Halloween I dressed up like a baby and he dressed up like my mother. In assembly he couldn't control himself and stood up on his seat, turned to the audience, and showed everyone his anatomically correct boobs. As his baby I had no choice but to grab them. We got big laughs but were both in trouble.

He had his own bike but never used it. He'd rather have

me pedal him around. He would sit on the seat and hold on to my belt loops and I would pedal him around town, through town centers, along wooded pathways, along the reservoir, up giants hills, while he was making me laugh so hard that it became impossible to balance. But rather than stop, he'd make me laugh harder, preferring to make us crash than stop laughing. He swore that one day he was going to get a moped and when he did he would ride me around on that.

I really had a brother.

In eighth grade we learned that he was being sent to the Catholic high school. We were going to be separated. That was a rough year. We started befriending other kids to bridge the gap. Rather than suffer a real hurt in the coming fall we unknowingly prepared ourselves by drifting apart.

We weren't at each other's homes every night anymore. We spent time with other kids. Made plans with other people. At the time I knew it was wrong to not always include him, and I'm sure he knew it too, but we were growing up and turning into people. Toughened-up, protected, calculating people.

The distance was especially obvious that last summer before school. There was nothing stopping us from doing all the things that we always had, but we no longer did. My parents would ask, "Where's Keith? We haven't seen him in a while." I'd mumble some answer in the way that kids do when they can't or don't really understand what's going on inside them. I was hurting but trying to survive at the same time.

The next year came and we went off to the scary world of high school. We called each other a couple times. At first there wasn't much to say. He was wrestling, I was playing football and we were making our way. But then, one night, it seemed like we came to the realization that people can be apart and be okay. That getting together, which was so natural not long ago, was now something we just had to plan. We were going to meet each other's new friends and we knew we'd like them. We made some dumb joke and laughed and I was so relieved and happy that maybe we'd return to the way we were.

I never saw him again.

I don't remember who told me. I don't remember even getting the news. I just remember trying to make sense of the flood of new words, many that were foreign to me, at age 14. Moped accident. Cargo van. Medivac. ICU. Head trauma. Wake. Closed casket. Funeral mass.

He was gone.

The funeral was filled with children. We were just children. Hundreds coming because he was in their class or on their team or in their school. There were so many children that I remember screaming in my head that I knew him more than all these other people. He was my friend. He wasn't theirs. He was mine. My brother. Why were they all here? To them he was a classmate, but to me he was so much more.

I never cried like that before. I never felt that grief before. I stood in my room with my father, a man who I never saw cry, holding on to my desk, sobbing. I smashed one of my shelves with my fist in rage. I simply didn't know what to do. I was lost. So young. So lost. And in a very real way I still am.

It never healed. Ever. It has been years since this happened. But it never changes.

My brother is gone.

aunts, uncles & cousins too

I have cousins coming out of my ears. I come from a large, Italian family. I'm one of twenty-one grandchildren, so that makes for a lot of cousins. You might think that I only saw them once a year at a family reunion, in some city park, like a normal family. Not Italians. We saw everybody, every Sunday, at my grandmother's house for dinner.

It was like having another set of friends who were picked for me by somebody else. They weren't like the kids I knew at school, they weren't as tight as siblings, they were somewhere in between. Sure, there were some weird ones, but we all got along because we had no choice, our parents made us.

Sometimes you have to put aside the patient rationalizing with children and just force them to do certain things. This goes beyond taking out the garbage and cleaning up their rooms. This includes the harder things they really don't want to do like loving the rest of the family.

Like an arranged marriage, we were told to love each other. The orders started with my grandmother and were passed along through every adult in the family, straight down to the children.

"There's no one more important than your family. Come give your grandmother a kiss. Say hello to your uncle. Kiss your cousin. Have you called your cousins? Are you getting together? Let Mark play the game with you two. Love each other. No one loves you more than your family. Get your finger out of your cousin's ear."

Things like this were said over and over again. We were brainwashed into loving one another and it worked. I call my cousins all the time and see them more than most of my friends. It's nice to know that I have this strange assortment of people, scattered all around the country, who have my back.

I now do the same thing with my children. I really believe that the reason my daughters get along with each other is because we didn't give them any choice.

"Be nice to your sister, she's your best friend. Love each other. Be nice to each other. Don't say that about your sister, she's the most important person in the world. Kiss your sister good night."

We watch other families let bad behavior toward their family slide and it ruins everything. The kids act nastily to one another and the parents just roll their eyes and wonder why they don't get along. Well, they don't get along because they haven't been taught to. They think it's okay to say something horrible about their sister or hit their brother. You have to stop this, at least when they're young. If they get older and they want to smack their brother around because he slept with his wife, stay out of it.

This was my grandmother's simple philosophy. Teach

the family to love the family. And we still do to this day. She also had another rule; that you should only clip your toe-nails after you get out of the shower because that's when they're softer. That one's not as deep but it's surprisingly just as true.

cool aunt vs.
creepy aunt

I love aunts. My aunts, your aunts, all aunts. How great are aunts? Aunts are the rodeo clowns of the family. They are the court jesters in a tense public court. They are the comic relief in a tense action drama. They are the furry little animated sidekick in a Disney film. They're good and crazy.

As a child, you recognize that they're just a little different from the other adults in the family. They're funny and weird and never discipline you. They're grown-ups who seem to have no authority and aren't interested in acquiring any. They have some kind of relationship with your parents but that has absolutely nothing to do with how they relate to you.

There are two general types of aunts: cool aunts and creepy aunts.

Cool aunts are something special. What makes them cool is that everything they do is cooler than your parents. This isn't difficult to achieve. Your parents are fried from spending every waking hour watching you, analyzing you, and wondering what they're doing wrong with you. Responsibility has worn them down to a parental nub.

On the other hand, cool aunts pride themselves on not

having any responsibility at all. They wear funny hats and drink big glasses of wine and say inappropriate things at the table. They bring weird boyfriends around once in a while who no one talks to, because they know they won't be around for long.

Aunts are more like children than adults, and to a kid that's just cool.

A cool aunt doesn't look at you as someone to discipline or teach. She knows as much about disciplining children as children do about retirement plans. She looks at you as someone to win over and she isn't above trying to buy your love. Knowing this is a huge advantage for a kid.

If your parents won't give you Doritos for breakfast, just ask your aunt. Do your parents say that video games are too violent? Your aunt doesn't care. You need some cash? Your aunt's got some and she's willing to give it to you because she knows that you're the closest thing to her own kids that she's going to get. And she's probably drunk. That's cool. That's like Keith Richards cool.

Sure, there's some competition for the coolest relative in the family. Grandma is always a steady favorite but can that old bag with the wobbly neck really compare? Let's see Grandma sneak you into an R-rated movie and drop major cash on popcorn and Sour Patch Kids. Grandma doesn't rock. Grandma naps.

A cool uncle is pretty close but a cool uncle is also dangerous. No one trusts that a cool uncle won't go over the line and turn a trip to the store into a long weekend in South Beach. No, the cool aunt knows how to walk the line. She wins.

Aunts have secrets too. Who really knows what your aunt does? She has a whole other life that she keeps hidden from the family. She has friends with exotic names and goes to wild places. She has a favorite dance club she frequents with a bunch of gay friends. She drinks during the day. She has a job that she doesn't talk about so you know it must be something strange.

Even the aunt with kids can be cool. She might have her own kids and she might even be strict with those kids, but she treats you differently. She knows what you're up to, she's seen it all before, but she'll let you slide. She's like a cop about to bust two drug dealers and you're the guy jaywalking across the street. She sees you but just can't be bothered right now.

Cool Aunt is great.

And then there's Creepy Aunt. This is the aunt who you really don't want to see and you definitely don't want to kiss hello. This is the aunt with weird hairs sticking out of that weird bubbly thing attached to her weird-shaped chin. This is the aunt who brings her own food in plastic containers because she has a lot of dietary restrictions. She smells like rose water and mothball soup.

Creepy Aunt drinks but tries to keep it a secret. She's not all goofy with a goblet of white wine like Cool Aunt. Creepy Aunt is into real-deal, serious drinking. She carries a worn silver flask attached to her leg with a garter belt. She doesn't drink from it, she takes snorts from it. Creepy.

She's the aunt who has weird-lady undergarments with strange straps and clasps that she hangs all around the bathroom after they've been floating in the sink. Creepy Aunt likes to hand wash things. Creepy.

If there's a cat lady in your family, chances are it's Creepy Aunt. Creepy Aunt doesn't even know how many cats she has because she's lost count. She just keeps opening cans of cat food and licking her fingers as more strays wander into her place. Creepy Aunt's apartment smells like kitty litter and old blankets and is covered in cat hair, but she likes all that hair, because when it sticks to her she thinks she looks a little like a cat herself.

Creepy Aunt is on a fixed income and doesn't want to spend money feeding you and quite frankly doesn't really want you around. That's okay, because you don't want to be left alone with Creepy Aunt, either. Maybe you ended up spending the night at Creepy Aunt's place when your parents ditched you, but that's a night you will not forget, neither of you enjoyed, and you will never repeat.

Unlike Cool Aunt, Creepy Aunt doesn't act like a kid, because she was never really a kid herself. She's the kind of person who at six years old would lean against the monkey bars and wonder why she was stuck with all these children. She's always been an adult and she thinks if you're standing up straight you must read the *New Yorker* and want to discuss Middle East politics. If you can't keep up with the conversation, she thinks you're stupid and sneaks off for another snort from her flask.

Creepy Aunt has secrets too, but hers are creepier. She has secrets about porcelain fairies and a collection of dirty old dolls that she talks to. What makes it even creepier is that she thinks they talk back.

The strange thing about Creepy Aunt is that you will probably come to appreciate her later in life. Because she doesn't know much about people your age, she will often give you a gift that means nothing to you as a child. But years later when you are packing or unpacking your belongings, you will find some great book that only now you understand and suddenly she makes sense. She was able to see "future you" and knew that one day you'd appreciate it. That's nice, but also, still creepy.

Either way, aunts are cool. Aunts are crazy. Aunts are out of their gourds. And they're a really fun part of the family. If you're really lucky you'll have two or three aunts who come together like the witches from *Macbeth* or the Marx Brothers in drag. They travel together in a boozy pack and are more fun than a box of kittens.

You know you're in for a good boozy time when somebody looks out the window and yells, "Mom, the aunts are here!"

uncle al,
all the kids' pal

Would you like to be popular? Do you want people to worship you? Become an uncle. The only way to be more popular is to be a dog, but let's stick with our own species. I was an uncle once. Technically, I'm still an uncle, but it's different now that I have children of my own. When I was single, all my focus was on my nieces and nephews, and I was a hell of a lot of fun.

My nephews looked at me and they knew three things: He has money, he has access to adult stuff, and he doesn't care what we do. And they were right. I would invite them, two at a time, to my apartment in New York and for two days we'd go nuts.

I saw it as my duty. How is a kid going to know what it feels like to eat Snickers bars and ice cream for breakfast if he never does it? The same went for R-rated movies, staying up till three A.M., and hanging out with comedians at a comedy club. These were all things they needed to know and it was up to me to show them.

I had a lot of uncles but, for the most part, they were a pretty tame crew. Uncle Rick was a good one. Dry, sarcastic, brutally funny, and he relentlessly teased my mother. These were all great qualities, but we never really did much together.

One of the only times we hung out was when he took me along while he played squash. It's a strange game; I'm not even sure if people play it anymore. You hit a hard, small ball with a badminton-type racket. It looks odd and a little awkward and that was how I felt when I had to join him in the men's locker room.

I can still picture the green, hard, vinyl tote bag that he gave me as a makeshift gym bag. It had a travel agent's logo on the side and a little white airplane and I remember it clearly because I just kept staring down at it, rather than at all these strange hairy men changing into their squash clothes.

That's a pretty lame memory but it's all I've got and I hold him responsible. He's a great guy to hang with as an adult, and we enjoy a nice cocktail together, but as a kid he wasn't that interesting.

I enjoyed my uncle Eddie. He was a funny storyteller. A really funny guy who would hold court in front of the entire family. He had real comic timing and a real ability to tell a story. Then he started drinking too much vodka and went through two divorces, lost his business, started saying inappropriate things about other races, and suddenly he wasn't so funny anymore.

Uncle Don was a good-natured lug with a really great laugh. Uncle Fred looked like a raven and was a very strict Catholic, so there was no way he was sneaking me into the movies to see *Animal House*.

They were all fine. Nice enough men, who led decent lives but in the "fun uncle department" were total flops.

And then there was Uncle Al.

Now, he was fun. While the other uncles were far off in a distant grown-up land, Uncle Al couldn't be bothered. He had served in Vietnam, ran a business during the tough Carter years, and had constant run-ins with dirty politicians in a corrupt city. He had met enough adults to be done with them all.

But kids he could relate to. Kids didn't lie to him about business deals, cheat him out of money, or try to take advantage of his good nature. Kids wanted the same things that he did: to screw around, have some fun, and not get caught.

When we were young he was fun in that playful-uncle kind of way. He was loaded with tricks. He'd steal things and make them reappear. He'd make his spaghetti slurp up into his mouth when he pressed the end of his nose. All the classics.

But when we got a little older that's when he got really fun. He would let us do all the things that our parents, and the law, thought we were too young for.

At family barbecues Uncle Al would sneak us beers. If he caught the older cousins smoking he would ask for one himself. He was always handing out cash like he was running for office. If he asked me to go to the store with him, there was a good chance that, at the age of fourteen, I'd be the one driving.

He was the best.

He loved dirty jokes and, unlike the other adults, didn't censor himself when he spoke to us. That's why kids love it when they hear adults curse, it shows that they're being honest. The other uncles talked differently to us kids which, in our minds, was tantamount to a lie.

He also smoked a lot of pot. He called marijuana his

"medicine" and from watching him manage his life it truly was. I'd see him pacing back and forth with a wrinkled brow, disappear out the back door, and return giggling and smiling like he'd just heard the best joke of his life.

He helped me buy my first car. I was determined to get my first car before I was old enough to drive. I worked for a couple years as a busboy in a restaurant called The Orchards. In keeping with its nature theme, not only were there pictures of trees on the walls and the chairs, but us busboys had to dress in all green. Green pants, apron, and bow tie. Like a leaf.

It was humiliating but for the first time in my life I was making money and I knew a car was within my reach. When I saved up about $1,200 there was only one person to call. Uncle Al.

He owned a junkyard. He didn't like that people called it a junkyard, but I don't know what else to call a giant yard filled with junky car parts. I asked if he knew of anything that I could afford.

"Sure, come down. I've got something you might like."

When I got there he was waiting for me in the parking lot with a 1976 Toyota Corolla. It was a fun-looking car, with a racing stripe down the side, as if anyone in a Corolla would be racing anything.

"What color would you say that is?" I asked.

"They call that baby-shit orange," said Uncle Al.

"Perfect."

I gave him the money and was on my way with my first car. All because of Uncle Al.

After several years, when the car eventually died on the side of the Garden State Parkway and I had to find a way to get it back home, again I called on Al.

I was distraught and saddened but he wouldn't allow that. He was laughing the whole way, saying that the engine was toast and that it might fall right out of the car in the middle of the road. Before long I was laughing too.

We barely got her back to the house and pushed it into the driveway. My beloved car was dead but that didn't mean that it was to be mourned. Especially with Al around. We lit a joint, said our goodbyes, and ate an entire sleeve of Oreos.

Al could fix anything. When I bought my first house Al was there all the time. He moved walls, installed a fireplace and a tile floor, ripped out an entire kitchen, and did endless smaller jobs that I couldn't handle. He was always happy to help, and during this time he was being treated for some blood ailment that made him tired and achy, but he didn't complain.

More than that, he would encourage me to sneak out with him and play golf whenever we could.

"Come on, Tommy, let's just say we're going for supplies," he'd say. Again, I drove.

He would sleep on this giant beanbag chair we had in the living room, sometimes staying for days before tackling the heinous drive through L.A. traffic back to his home in San Diego.

We've lost touch a little in recent years. He moved to South Carolina and my work life has me continually pinned to the ground. But we had some great times and the relationship we had was the type of honest relationship that can only come from an uncle. Hopefully I've achieved a little of that with my nieces and nephews and in the future when we aren't together as much, hopefully we'll still be connected too.

As with all the important people in our lives, we can't live with them forever but they will always live within us. At least that's what it feels like after I've had a little of Uncle Al's medicine.

cool things to do with your uncle when you're young

Smoke a Pack of Camels
Go to R-Rated Movies
Play Video Games in a Bar
Mix His Martinis
Shuck Oysters
Melt Things with a Blowtorch
Open His Beers with a Quarter
Clean His Gun
Enjoy Unsupervised Late-Night Internet Access
Drive

your cousins will
ruin your life

This is a story about why it's not a good idea to smoke pot with your cousins when you're ten.

When I was ten, a lot of the older cousins were starting to get married. This was a big deal for us younger cousins because up until then, all our parties involved birthday cakes and pinning a tail on a donkey.

Now we were around dance floors, drunk adults, and cool older kids. My cousin Robert and I really wanted to be included with the older cousins, especially the ones who would always sneak out of the weddings to go do what must have been even cooler stuff. We had no idea where they went but we badly wanted to go.

We showed up to the next wedding looking really cool. We leaned against the bar in our little-man suits, throwing back a couple Shirley Temples, trying to get noticed. And noticed we were, by our two older cousins, David and Jimmy. They gave us that cool-guy, head-nod thing that was the first step to going outside with them. This was totally cool; we were very excited and fought really hard not to show it.

We approached.

"You two maggots want to come with us?"

"Sure. We were just gonna finish these drinks, but . . ."

"Now."

"Okay."

"Don't tell nobody."

We followed them out of the wedding hall, trying to look like we were on official business, and we were on our way.

"Where are we going?"

"To my car."

"Wow, you drove yourselves?" asked Robert.

"What do you think, dweeb?"

I punched Robert in the arm. Two feet from the front door and he was already blowing it. We'd never be asked along again if he kept spitting out comments like that. Total dweeb.

They opened the doors to the Chevy Nova and got in.

"No, you guys can't get in, there's no back seat. Just lean in the window."

So we each put the top half of our body into the car as they rolled the windows up, trapping us, with our little ties dangling, as Jimmy took a bunch of weed out of the glove compartment and started rolling a joint on a magazine.

I had never seen marijuana before and I was scared and freaking out and trying to look like this wasn't a big deal.

"Have you ever gotten high?" they asked Robert.

I shot him a look.

"Totally. I've gotten so many highs before," Robert said.

"Me too, so many times. It's not a big deal," I added.

They grinned knowingly at each other as they lit up the joint and proceeded to get us high the same way stoners get their dogs high. They blew it in our faces and laughed. If you've ever wondered if a dog can get high that way, I can tell you from experience that yes, they can. Very high.

"Is this how you got high last time?"

"Yeah, just like this."

"Me too. It's no big deal," I said as I coughed and choked at the same time.

When they were done messing with us, they rolled down the windows and let us go.

"You guys can't walk in with us, you'll get us caught. Go around the back."

"Totally. That's how we did it last time."

"What are you talking about?" I whispered.

"I don't know."

"Me neither."

We started laughing and trying to walk in our hard dress shoes that felt like ice skates on the parking lot. We looked like two little drunk businessmen heading back to the hotel after a sales convention dinner.

Neither of us had ever done anything like this before. We had no idea that this was what went on. We just thought that we were going to play catch or sit on the curb like the cool kids at school. We had no idea we were following two drug addicts to the underworld.

As we walked around the back we managed to do something that is pretty impossible while walking around a single building: We got lost. Somehow we ended up on the edge of a golf course not knowing which way to turn, and not caring anymore either, because suddenly we were faced with the greenest grass we had ever seen. It was a dazzling field shimmering full of smiling sunlight. I was really high.

To add to the magical feel of the experience a deer peacefully emerged from the woods and began gently nibbling at the grass. She was so perfectly natural and for a moment it seemed as if everything in the whole world folded into complete silence.

"Look, a horse!" said Robert. "Let's catch it!"

"I don't think that's a . . ."

"Come on!" Robert said as he took off, leaving me no choice but to start running along with him.

"Ahhhhh!"

We were screaming and running like two drunk, Japanese businessmen sprinting to karaoke. The deer started to run away, leaping through the trees, but after a few steps she just stopped. She turned toward us as if she suddenly realized what was chasing her: two idiots.

We stopped too, and for a beat the three of us stood frozen, like we were watching a movie and couldn't figure out what was going to happen next.

As my cousin leaned in and whispered, "Do you think we can eat it?" the deer ran right for us. She was charging and not the way a deer normally runs, but up on her back legs, like a person.

"Killer horse!" screamed Robert. "Ahhhh!"

I have never been so scared in all my life. She was coming right for us with her front hooves spinning like a buzz saw. I didn't know what was happening. This was all new. We were ten, we were high, and now we were screaming in our suits, running for our lives. We were so hysterical with fear and laughter that our legs didn't work. We fell on the muddy ground, grabbing onto each other, arms flailing, half crying, our mouths filled with dirt and leaves. The deer closed in on us.

"We're dead!" screamed Robert.

As we lay there in a ball on the ground, the deer stomped all around us, like she took pity on these two blubbering mini accountants. When Robert wet his pants and we were deemed no longer a threat, she returned her hooves to the ground, gave us one last look, and calmly walked off.

"Good horsey," cried Robert.

We pulled and crawled our way out of the trees and made our way up to the patio of the club and collapsed on a lounge chair.

"Where were you two?" asked my father as he grabbed us by our mini lapels.

"We were attacked by a horse," I said.

"Don't lie to me. Your cousins are in there telling everyone you were smoking pot."

"No way."

"Never."

"Well, stay away from your cousins. They may look like fun, but they're potheads who will ruin your lives."

He marched back inside and we realized we were safe. We weren't getting in trouble and that horse thing wasn't going to eat us. We looked at each other in our mud-caked suits and laughed harder than we ever had, or ever would, again.

strangers

Even a large family isn't really that many people. A friend of mine is one of ten children and, while it sounds like a crazy place to grow up, if you took those same people and put them in a Costco, the place would feel pretty empty. The fact is, out of the billions of people running around looking for lunch, you deal with a ridiculously small sampling.

These people aren't just strangers, they're bit players, cast as extras in your movie. But if the script were just slightly different they could've been main characters. That guy across the aisle on the plane, with the weird chin beard, he could have been your husband. That woman in the all-pink outfit, who cut the line at the dry cleaners, could have been someone on your Christmas list. And that old dude who is clipping his fingernails on the subway could have been your dad! Thankfully, he's not, but he could have been and hopefully you would make him stop the inappropriate grooming.

I see all of these people when I tour and get to talk to a lot of them too. I'm not going to chat you up on the airplane, but if you have a story to tell, I don't mind listening. I learn a lot from these folks, like the guy who taught me how to clean the smudges off my eyeglasses and the lady who showed me that it's possible to wear a bra on the outside of her jacket.

Here are some who I've met along the way. Some are great, some are crazy, but I'm better off having met them and even better off when I waved goodbye to them.

rocky road

I met a woman today. She's a waitress in a roadside kitchen that is only open for breakfast and lunch. She is a short, husky woman in her early fifties, one of those people who looks like she had a really good time in the eighties. There's a faded tattoo on her arm and a raspy, *I used to smoke, well, I still kind of smoke, mostly I just smoke when I'm drinking* kind of voice.

I was in Wickenburg, Arizona, to do a show at a performing arts center there. It's an old cowboy town with a lot of retired people who have money but don't like to flaunt it. They dress in faded, dusty jeans and worn-out cowboy boots. It's a friendly place, the kind of place that is very American but very far from the rest of the country at the same time, and that's why they live there.

She was wrapping up for the day along with another waitress and the owner. I was the last customer in the place and as we got to talking they found out I was a comedian and got a little excited to share things that they thought were funny.

When I was younger I found this a little annoying, but like many things in my life, I realized it's best not to fight what constantly comes my way and have since embraced it. And why shouldn't I? My job is gathering stories from different points of view and translating what I find into what I think is funny. If someone wants to offer that up, I might as well give them the chance.

I had mistakenly ordered a gigantic double cheeseburger. I say it was a mistake because after two hours of highway travel I couldn't focus on the menu. I could feel her impatience grow as she stood over me with her pad, and in a desperate move I just blurted out the first thing I could read. She was happy that I ordered her favorite and even happier that I was doing a really good job getting through it. That's when she decided to tell a story that she assumed I, a fellow aggressive eater, could relate to.

"Here's a funny one for you."

People start this way a lot, as if they think they are giving me a gift, which I guess they are but, like most gifts you get in life, very few are good enough to hang on to.

"I bought some Rocky Road ice cream the other day. You know how you're driving down the road and, all of a sudden, you just have to get some Rocky Road so bad that you pull right into the supermarket, march in, and get some?" she asked.

I nodded along, but I didn't know what she meant exactly. I have had cravings for food but never so strong and immediate that I involuntarily cut across three lanes of traffic to satisfy it.

"So I brought it home and put it in the freezer but I got busy and kind of forgot about it. I guess just buying it and knowing it was in the house was enough. So I woke up in the middle of the night and you know how sometimes you just wake up out of a dead sleep and you just have to have a bowl of Rocky Road?"

I said, "Sure," but, again, I had no idea what she was talking about.

The average American doesn't go to bed hungry, and the idea that I would just pop up out of a dead sleep and stumble to the kitchen for a bowl of ice cream, like a sleepwalking crazy person, was lost on me.

That kind of behavior is from a different time. *Dagwood* was a famous comic strip during the postwar years that featured a skinny guy who ate giant stacked sandwiches as a midnight snack. But this was a fantasy of an America that was really hungry and hardly had any food at home. Today we consider these Dagwood monstrosities to be a normal-sized sandwich. But who am I to judge? She said she was hungry.

"So I just went down there and fixed me up a bowl of Rocky Road. It wasn't a huge bowl but I really filled it up. I just love Rocky Road."

"Seems like it."

"So I took it to bed with me and the next thing I know it's morning, but when I wake up my eyes won't open. They're stuck shut. I don't know what's going on. I thought I must've been bit by a spider, again. So I start rubbing them and they slowly open and when I look down it looks like I am covered in blood. My arms and my chest are just covered and I think I must have been stabbed in the middle of the night."

"Yikes."

"I know. I am freaking out, so I take a Xanax to calm myself down because I don't know what the hell is going on. I think someone came in and tried to kill me but I don't feel no hole or nothing. And then I see the bowl on the bed. And this is the funny part," she said.

A lot of people say this as well. They point out when the funny part is coming. I understand this. It happens when you are starting to feel that maybe the story, when told out loud, might not be as funny as you thought. This one wasn't hilarious but I was definitely into it.

"I must have gotten back into bed, took one bite and fell right asleep. I was covered in Rocky Road. You know how when Rocky Road dries it looks just like dried blood and gets all dark brown?"

"Yes, I do."

"Well, that's what it looked like. I started laughing and I took a picture of myself and sent it off to my daughter at college. She was in class and she gets my picture and immediately started crying and had to run out to the hall and call me because it looked like I had been in an accident. When I told her it was ice cream, she said I had issues and I told her, 'I ain't got no issues, you should be happy for me. Your mama got lucky last night with a bowl of Rocky Road!' Now ain't that funny?" she asked.

"It really is," I said.

And I wasn't lying.

I liked her attitude. She was enjoying herself, had some grown kids running around while she was hustling at this restaurant to keep her life afloat, and occasionally dove into a bowl of Rocky Road.

I'm not sure what happened to her husband but he obviously wasn't sharing a bed with her any longer. Maybe a similar thing had happened early on in their relationship with a different food or maybe it happened repeatedly and is partly the cause of their breakup.

Either way, that story actually was a gift that I have kept with me. And now I give it to you.

Funny, right?

new americans

We live in a great, big, ever-changing country, with new types
of people emerging all the time. It's good to keep an eye on the
emerging trends, as there's a constant back-and-forth between
our families and the culture. Most of the people will never
cross your path, but then again they might marry your sister.
As I glide through airports and shopping malls with my mental
notepads, these are a few of the new groups I have observed.

trolls

We have heard of internet trolls, despicable people who slither
along the net, spewing hateful comments at innocent people
who are just looking for a funny video or a challah bread recipe.
Well, they are no longer anonymous. I see them. They are here
in the airport with me right now. The giveaway: They look
like actual trolls, if trolls were actual beings, and from what I
can see on this Starbucks line, they are.

They are mainly white guys with little raisin, shame-filled
eyes that peek out from beneath the dirty wool hats that they
wear year-round. They stagger around on stubby, rounded

legs, with their shoulders hunched over from their constant, downward, cellular gaze.

They have pudgy noses and long, unkempt beards that grow out of their splotchy, sun-starved skin. These aren't well-groomed hipster beards and artisanal mustaches. These are grown from years of neglect, giving them the straggly look of creatures who live under a bridge or in a mushroom patch.

They have little potbellies filled with cheeses and sausages and yeasty beers named after dogs and obscure mountain ranges. They have round, meaty hands that they use to pick their noses and stick in their pants, which they often do in crowds, thinking if they don't look at other people, then the others can't see them. But I see them, lurking over their laptops and smartphones, spewing out obscenities with those same dirty hands.

If you get close to them, they smell like old ham and corn chips. When they breathe out, their breath is reminiscent of the inside of a barn, filled with dirty livestock.

The adult acne on their faces proves that they don't wash very often and the stains on their worn-out shirts show that, with all the time they spend online, laundry day doesn't happen too often.

I imagine that their beds are constructed like a rat's nest out of newspaper clippings, used tissues, foam food containers, soy sauce packets, and other materials that they were able to shave down into nesting material with their pointy teeth.

They don't come out of their dens too often, but when they do they are easy to spot if you know what to look for. There's no need to fear them, but at the same time don't get too close or you could catch some ancient, reptilian disease for which there is no cure.

techno-idiots

Technology is all around us—saving people's lives, curing blindness, enabling the elderly to breathe, and exposing troublemakers around the globe. Technology is powerful and exciting unless, of course, it is in the hands of idiots.

There is an idiot sitting near me in this car wash waiting area, right now. I picked out a quiet seat, next to the brochure display, and all was well until this woman marched into this oasis with her smartphone on speaker. Speaker! So we can all hear the even louder woman on the other end of this call, who can't believe what her boyfriend said to her last night.

This is a techno-idiot.

It is a rare thing to find silence anywhere in this country. Everywhere I go there are leaf blowers, car horns, and airplanes roaring up above. All of which make the added noise of techo-idiots blabbering away on phones, playing music without earbuds, and letting their "It's Raining Men" ringtone go off in the library all that much worse.

These people must be stopped and we must be the ones to stop them. If they are breaking the social norms of quiet space, then we should be allowed to spray them with water bottles, toss French fries at them, and let our dogs loose when they pass by.

the super sports fan

Human beings are tribal. Since the days of living in caves and eating farm-to-table woolly mammoths, we tend to seek out and stay with like-minded groups. This has helped form com-

munities and book clubs, but it can also make us alienate anyone who is different from us. In extreme cases this separation
from others can turn violent and erupt into conflict and war.

The replacement for this aggression in our modern culture
is sports. Thank God for football, basketball, hockey, and
baseball. They really do so much more than people realize.

If you don't like sports and you find watching them a waste
of time, I get it. There are millions of people who crossed
paths with jocks while growing up, and they were the sole
cause of their unhappiness. But that is exactly why you should
be thankful that sports exist.

Without them, these packs of wild men would literally
be running through your towns looking for fights. If the
Pittsburgh Steelers and the Cleveland Browns weren't around,
filling their stadiums with eighty thousand fans, what do you
think those barbarians would do with their idle time?

Steeler fans would organize, make a flag, get some uniforms,
and hold meetings about those awful sons-of-bitches in Cleveland. Then they would get drunk, buy weapons, and load into
cars and head to Lake Erie. Not to an organized stadium, but
to the streets, where they would drag people out of their homes
and beat them with wooden planks.

Thank God for the NFL.

And so now we have super fans, those fellow citizens you
see walking around dressed like the players. They wear jer-
seys, hats, and colored socks and paint their faces and torsos.
What is this, if not war regalia? They identify with these
teams. They research the enemy. They bleed the team colors.
Without this they would be bleeding real blood and ours
would somehow be in the mix.

Let them buy bumper stickers for their cars and banners

for their homes. Let them play dress-up and scream at the TV. Let them stand for hours in parking lots, eating cooked meat and getting drunk from cans of beer, mocking fans in different colors.

Is there anything wrong with these people? I say no. They come from a certain warrior line of DNA. They are the soldiers who fought the necessary fights that protected families and formed cities and towns. They weren't pretty back then, they're not pretty now and that's the point. They're not looking for acceptance, they're looking for a fight. So be grateful they're screaming at Tom Brady and not you.

the angry, middle-aged white guy

There are millions of middle-aged white guys, but the thing that sets this new group apart is the anger. These guys are pissed off. They are angry at young people, they are angry at women, they are angry at just about everybody. They are even angry at other angry middle-aged white guys.

You can spot them because they have stopped caring about how they look. They wear the one pair of jeans they bought twenty years ago and a dirty baseball hat with the logo of a tool company or fish on it. They all have the same potbelly and faded T-shirt they got for free from a thing a long time ago. They don't shave very often and their white whiskers look like cactus spikes against their sunburned faces.

They get in the car and start calling other drivers names before they even pull out of the driveway. They think everyone is a moron driving around like an idiot just to mess with them. As far as they're concerned everyone on the road drives too fast, too slow, and are too stupid to get out of the way.

Everyone is the enemy. The slow cashier. The cops. The neighbors. The Mexicans. The Muslims. The weather. Squirrels. The neighbor's dog. The neighbor's cat. The neighbor's kids. Traffic. Lines. Stores. Music. TV shows. Commercials. Politicians. Waiters. The phone company. The cable company. The TSA. The airlines. The EPA. Girl Scouts. Time. Their penis. Reading glasses. Apps that ask for passwords. Computers. Rain. Sun. God. Their wives. Their children. And the New York Yankees.

These guys are really pissed off.

This is what happens when you win too much. You win your whole life, you think it's going to last forever, but eventually you get old and life ends up on top. It's the one time when being white in America isn't an advantage and they've decided to go down swinging.

What they fail to realize is that it's not the world conspiring against them, it's their own mortality. No matter how angry they get and how many dinner parties they ruin with their angry rants, they can't turn back the clock. Life is too short to be that angry.

So when you see them coming, it's best just to get out of their way. They'll find someone or something else to be angry with. And if they're coming over for Thanksgiving, do your best to sit at the other end of the table, and don't let anyone discuss *anything*.

hot moms

If you have ever gone to a back-to-school night or been caught in line at at carpool, you have run into a new kind of mom. The Hot Mom. They are youthful, attractive, and should be stopped.

You should see the moms at my kids' school. It's like a competition. They must get up at five in the morning to get ready so they can be the Hot Mom. But here is the thing: Some dads might be interested, a few mothers a little jealous, but no kid wants their mom to be hot.

When you're a kid, you don't want a hot mom, you want a blend-in mom. Just a flowered housedress and wobbly bingo-arms mom. Big sloppy mom boobs that you can curl up in, like a cinnamon-scented beanbag chair. That's a mom. She's warm and cuddly and makes kick-ass mac and cheese.

And I have news for you, if you are the Hot Mom: The other moms aren't calling you hot. They're calling you a whore.

know-nothing life masters

These are young couples who haven't done anything but for some reason think they know everything about life. I was sitting on a beach next to a pair and they were talking about how they're going to raise their children when they have them one day.

"I just think that it's important that they know you love them," she said. "So when I come home, anytime I walk in the door I am going to put down my bags, sit on the floor, and hold them for five straight minutes. Because, like, a child needs to know that you care more about them than you do about all this other stuff going on in the world. So like, that would be my rule, like every time I come home. Like, I just don't know why more parents don't do that."

If you have kids, and you have thrown this book against the wall, walked around the block a couple times, and have returned, welcome back.

Can you imagine how little this woman knows about being the head of a family? As if the only reason you don't give your child all of your attention the minute you walk in the door is because you are selfish. How about the fact that when you walk in the door the kids are screaming, the dog is biting the babysitter, and, if you don't make dinner and feed everyone in the next ten seconds, everyone's schedule is off and they won't get to bed on time, and oh, yeah, everyone has the stomach flu.

The thing they talked about next really put me over the top. And it's not just the subject matter and the complete lack of knowledge that made me want to throw them into traffic. It was that arrogant tone that condescends to everyone on the planet but them. That half-whining, self-involved cadence that sounds like they just woke up and ends everything with a little bit of a question mark even though they aren't asking at all.

"I think I want to get a dog first, because it's just like a child," he said. "But I don't want a little dog, like a pug; screw pugs."

"Pugs are gross."

"Yeah. And then my brother was telling me to get a pure breed, because you know what you're getting, but I feel like there are so many dogs out there who need help, you know?" he said as he sipped his cold brew before going on.

"Have you heard of wolf dogs? They are part dog and part wolf and they're pretty amazing but have, like, this really bad reputation because people don't know how to treat them? And I just feel like I would be the type of person, I mean, I never had a dog, but I feel like I would be really good with a wolf dog. Like, I would be able to understand them more than other people."

All I could think was, *Please get a wolf dog. Please. I would love nothing more than for you to get a wolf dog and when your girlfriend comes home and sees that it ate her boyfriend, we'll see if she still drops what she's doing and sits on the floor for five minutes to let it know she loves it.*

people to avoid on a plane

Anyone Clipping Their Nails
The Guy with His Feet in the Magazine Pouch
Babies
Anyone with McDonald's Takeout
The Toddler with an iPad and No Earbuds
Homemade Tuna Fish Sandwich Guy
The Girl with the Chihuahua in a BabyBjörn
The Drooler
Flight Attendants
Kim Jong-Un

and, finally . . .
just eat the bread

Good job; you've reached the end! Even if you've skipped some pages, I'm proud of you. And, as a token of my appreciation, I am going to give you this final, simple advice for a happy life: Just eat the bread.

When they bring out the basket and put it on the table, don't make a big deal out of it. Don't make a face. Don't yell at the waiter and make him take it back. Just eat the bread. You deserve it.

I don't want you to deny yourself this little innocent pleasure anymore. I have friends who don't eat bread. In a masochistic campaign against all things human and joyful, they have sworn off bread. When someone tells me they don't eat bread I have to ask, "Why are you even here?"

Not only do I eat the bread, but I bake the bread. All the time. A lot of bread. I bake bread, feed the ones I love, and share it with everyone I know. I fill the house with the smells of fresh-baked bread. I have my children coming into the kitchen, opening the bread bin, and looking for more bread. They call me on the road and ask when I'm coming home, not because they want to see me but because they want more bread. Everyone is happier.

We have grilled cheese. We have avocado toast. We have paninis. We have bread with our eggs. We have bread with our pasta. We love bread. Bread is good. Bread is life. Bread is delicious. Who doesn't love bread? We all love bread. So why would you stop eating bread?

Did you do something wrong? Are you in need of discipline? Do you need to be taught a lesson? No. You are living your life and a life is not a life unless it has the very basic enjoyments, and one of the really big ones is eating bread.

Not eating bread is a symptom of a much larger problem: that we are all caught in this anxiety-filled life that constantly creates the feeling that you're not good enough. You are good enough, you're doing great. Are there struggles and challenges? Of course there are; you just read a whole book about them. That's a part of life and so is bread. It's your reward.

Bread is good. Human beings have been happily eating bread for thousands of years. Why are you taking out all of your worries and low self-esteem on this innocent, delightful food? Don't you think there are better places to put your blame?

How about glucose and sugar and high-fructose corn syrup? How about that box of Cheez-Its, that Ben & Jerry's, and those Kettle chip people? And the Coke and Diet Coke and Diet Dr Pepper people? They make highly refined salt-, fat-, and sugar-delivery systems designed to addict you and keep you coming back for more. Bread is made from flour,

282 | your dad stole my rake

water, salt, and yeast. That's it. No monoglycerides, calcium propionate, datem, lecithin, and potassium sorbate. Don't eat potassium sorbate, eat bread.

I don't want to live in a world of people who act like a wrap is the same as a sandwich. Who don't put butter on toast. What are you going to soak the tomato sauce up with? What are you going to put your grilled cheese on? There are people out there wrapping their cheeseburgers in lettuce leaves. Stop it. That's not a cheeseburger. That's meat in a leaf.

Why punish yourself for not having the body of an Olympic athlete? You don't have the body of an Olympic athlete because you're not an Olympic athlete! You are the guy who works at the construction company. You're the construction company guy. You don't need a rocking bod, you need a tool belt.

Just eat the bread.

You're a mom. You care for the family and you are loved and adored. You don't need a six-pack. No one would want to see it if you had it. We're not interested in that. We're interested in you and what you have to say and what you are doing and the advice you give. If you have abs, we know that you're not spending enough time thinking about the important things in life, namely us, the family.

Eat the bread.

You need to give yourself a break and enjoy your life. You aren't going to turn into a monster if you eat bread. You are going to be you. Always you. Just a happier version of you.

I know it's difficult to treat yourself well, so I am officially giving you permission to eat it. And because I think you are doing so well in your life, please find (below) a signed permission slip you can present to whoever gets in your way. I am also including some other permission slips for you to cut out, hold up high, and tell everyone that you have been rewarded for doing the best you can. And that's all you can do.

Thanks for reading and enjoy.

acknowledgments

I would like to acknowledge the following people and pets who not only helped me with this book but who inspired, advised, and listened to me talk about the process of writing over cocktails and coffee.

Let's eliminate the suspense we feel during award shows when we are waiting to see if the winner remembers to thank their spouse and start off with my wife, Cynthia. From the beginning she has been my friend and my muse. This may sound romantically poetic, but when you are the muse of a stand-up comedian it means having to hear things from your personal life told in comedy specials, theaters, and late-night talk shows. Thankfully, she has an amazing sense of humor and an amazing laugh. I love you.

My children are an inspiration but more than that they are a distraction from all the lame things that nag at me from the adult world. It's so great to sit with people who don't know when their appointments are, what they have to do that day, and how much anything costs. You keep me young. Don't grow up. I'm serious.

The rest of my family, my amazing parents, Tom and Elaine,

who continue to give me amazing material, camera-shy sisters Jennifer and Kristin, cousins, aunts, and uncles, I think about you all every day and now I have written about most of you. I wish we saw each other more often.

My publisher, the amazing Elizabeth Beier, who has been a great guide and friend and who I know I will be eating many more long, interesting meals with. Nicole Williams and all the staff at St. Martin's Press for taking care of all the details that I can't begin to keep track of.

My trusty book agent, Richard Abate, who got the thing made and makes me want to write another book because he truly knows what funny is.

The creative influences in my life are long and impactful and it almost seems silly to just list you all. But you should know that I consider myself extremely lucky to have met you, worked with you, and that we are friends. Unless you have passed, in which case I feel like I hardly even knew thee. My life is filled with some of the most amazing people and it's not a coincidence that they're all funny.

Estee Adoram, Max Burgos, Dave Becky, Noam Dworman, Matt Damon, Greg Jacobs, Mark "Flanny," Flanagan Ava Harel, Jim Harrison, Garrison Keillor, Josh Leiberman, Keith Potter, Kevin Potter, Jim Gaffigan, Greg Giraldo, Jane Lynch, Alfred E. Newman, Jerry Seinfeld, Steven Soderbergh, Daniel Tosh, John Updike, Colin Quinn, Walt Whitman, Baby, Bella, Bowser, Gracie, Biggleswade.

Thank you all.

tom gave me permission to

leave the dishes in the sink

tom gave me permission to

buy bigger pants

tom gave me permission to

go to a movie
during the day

tom gave me permission to

have ice cream for dinner

tom gave me permission to

let the kids skip practice

tom gave me permission to

eat more bread